Buckinghamshire
and East Berkshire
40 favourite walks

The author and publisher have made every effort to ensure that the information in this publication is accurate, and accept no responsibility whatsoever for any loss, injury or inconvenience experienced by any person or persons whilst using this book.

published by
pocket mountains ltd
The Old Church, Annanside,
Moffat DG10 9HB

ISBN: 978-1-916739-14-7

Text and photography copyright © Ben Giles 2026

The right of Ben Giles to be identified as the Author of this work has been asserted by him in accordance with the Copyright, Designs and Patents Act 1988

A catalogue record for this book is available from the British Library

Contains Ordnance Survey data © Crown copyright and database 2026

All rights reserved. No part of this publication may be reproduced, stored in a retrieval system, or transmitted in any form or by any means, electronic or mechanical, including photocopying and recording, unless expressly permitted by Pocket Mountains Ltd.

Printed by J Thomson Colour Printers, Glasgow

Introduction

Of all the counties surrounding London, Buckinghamshire and Berkshire are often most closely associated with the title 'home counties' and both still contain large stretches of what is thought of by many as quintessential English countryside. While these two counties may not contain dramatic soaring hills, expanses of high moorland, great towering sea cliffs, or the depths of gorge-like valleys, there are woods and fields, rivers and streams, and open air in abundance. The Chilterns dominate the south of Buckinghamshire, a plateau-like maze of chalk hills covered with beechwoods, villages and fields rising from the Thames Valley to a steep northern escarpment. At its foot dotted with villages and criss-crossed by streams, the fertile farmland of the Vale of Aylesbury stretches northwards towards the River Great Ouse and the start of the Midlands beyond. Southwards, across the River Thames lies Berkshire. While more built-up than its northern neighbour, the east of the county still has some exquisite countryside – the landscaped parkland of Windsor Castle, the stretch enclosed by the loop of the Thames between Maidenhead and Reading, and the wooded expanse of Swinley Forest which borders on Hampshire.

Many of the smaller towns and villages in Buckinghamshire and Berkshire, particularly those bordering on Greater London, have become increasingly suburbanised and the capital forever pushes its western limits further outwards, yet the green belt still casts a protective ring and has preserved much of the area's traditional landscape character. Nevertheless, year on year pressure for housing and for living space continually threatens to extend already densely populated conurbations. But keener too is the desire for respite from the busyness of life and the clear need for green spaces close to home. And if we think that in the 21st century we are hemmed in and busier as never before, perhaps some comfort can be taken that, though undoubtedly more acute than ever, this idea is not new and has a long history in this part of England.

More than 200 years ago, the poet William Cowper experienced such disorientation and sought a quieter life at Olney in the north of Buckinghamshire. Though his fame has faded, he was one of the best known poets of his time, feted by both Samuel Taylor Coleridge and William Wordsworth for his poems on nature and country life. Cowper spoke of nature as a 'blest seclusion from a jarring world'. This struck a chord in the 20th century with the landscape artist John Nash, who was likewise a resident of Buckinghamshire and a frequent visitor to the Chilterns. In the 1930s Nash was commissioned by the poet John Betjeman and the artist John Piper to write the original *Shell Guide to Buckinghamshire* and

The River Thames near Hurley ▶

it was no coincidence that he ended his introduction to the guide by quoting Cowper's famous line. A more distant example can also be found even further back during the time of the Great Plague in the second half of the 17th century, when John Milton, often considered the most celebrated of English poets after William Shakespeare, took refuge from London in the then secluded Buckinghamshire village of Chalfont St Giles, in a small cottage now open to the public. Here, away from the world of politics in the turbulent aftermath of the English Civil War, Oliver Cromwell's Commonwealth and the Restoration of Charles II, he was able to complete his masterpiece *Paradise Lost* and was inspired to begin work on its sequel, *Paradise Regained*.

About this guide

This guide contains 40 routes ranging in length from a short stroll to a good half-day's walking, divided into four sections, three covering Buckinghamshire and one for East Berkshire, broadly based on the topography of the region. All of the routes are circular and are intended as comfortable walks or strolls. On a few routes the cumulative ascent or some steeper slopes in the Chilterns may require greater exertion than the strict route length suggests, but in general the walking is on well-worn paths, lanes and tracks, with plenty of waymarks, which should require minimal time and effort for route-finding. The route descriptions concentrate on the salient points of navigation, but may not cover every twist or turn. If in doubt, the obvious path is usually the line to take. In addition, the

accompanying sketch maps serve an illustrative purpose and, for the longer or more complex routes, it would be a good idea to have access to the relevant OS Explorer mapping, details of which are given at the start of each walk.

The recommended time for each walk is an estimate based on an average walking speed of 4kmph, with a small allowance added in on some hillier routes. However, timings will vary significantly, not only for individuals but also given the seasonal effects on paths, especially those crossing fields, or tracks in the Chilterns, sections of which can become muddier and more slippery at certain times of year. A few routes also pass along rivers, sections of which can be liable to flooding. Most paths covered in the routes are well-used and well-maintained by local agencies but, in spring and summer especially, hedges and undergrowth grow vigorously and nettles, brambles and thorn can infiltrate narrower paths, stile crossings and gates. Signage of rights of way in both Buckinghamshire and East Berkshire is generally very good, especially on waymarked routes such as the Thames Path and the Ridgeway. It is hoped that there is plenty of interest along the routes themselves and it would be possible to spread a short walk over half a day if time is taken to explore along the way. In addition, this volume's companion *Oxfordshire and West Berkshire: 40 Town & Country Walks* provides further scope for exploring the region on foot.

Getting around and access

Many of the towns in Buckinghamshire and East Berkshire can serve as useful bases for walking. In the northern half of

◀ Looking westwards from Coombe Hill to Beacon Hill

Buckinghamshire the main towns are Buckingham and Aylesbury, with Milton Keynes near its borders with Northamptonshire and Bedfordshire. In the west, just over the county border, lie the smaller towns of Brackley, Bicester and Thame, while in the south and east are Princes Risborough, High Wycombe, Amersham and Beaconsfield. Reading is the county town of Berkshire and to its east lie the conurbations of Wokingham and Bracknell, Maidenhead, and Slough, with Windsor at the county's eastern limit.

Buckinghamshire is served by the M40, the major motorway running northwestwards between London and Birmingham, while Berkshire is served by the M4 heading westwards to Bristol. The very busy M25 also skirts the east of Buckinghamshire and the M1 passes to the north of Milton Keynes, while the M3 gives access to some southern stretches of East Berkshire. All these routes are major transport links and can become busy at peak times and during holidays.

A good number of the main towns in both counties have railway stations, where services are run by Chiltern Railways between London and Birmingham and by Great Western Railway between London and Bristol. In addition, Amersham and Chesham are connected to the London Underground network by the Metropolitan line. Regular bus routes serve all the main towns and an effort has been made to start walks from places which are served by public transport. However, it is worth noting

◀ Hurley Church

that it is increasingly the case that many villages in rural areas are only intermittently served by public bus on both a weekly or seasonal basis. Access by car is still the preferred option for many and, while towns cater adequately for parking, this can be a sensitive issue in smaller villages and hamlets. Pubs and inns can be very accommodating if the intention is to visit before or after a walk but where parking is outside designated car parks, consideration should be shown for the needs and access of local residents and the farming community.

Outside the major conurbations, Buckinghamshire and, to a lesser extent, East Berkshire are still substantially rural. At lambing time, signs on gates may well request that dogs are kept on a lead and the presence of dogs for cows can be problematic – it is not unheard of for cows with calves to behave in a very protective way. Even without a dog, cattle just released from winter shelters or cows which have recently calved should be left well alone. If in doubt, it is usually advisable and possible to find a short detour to avoid such livestock.

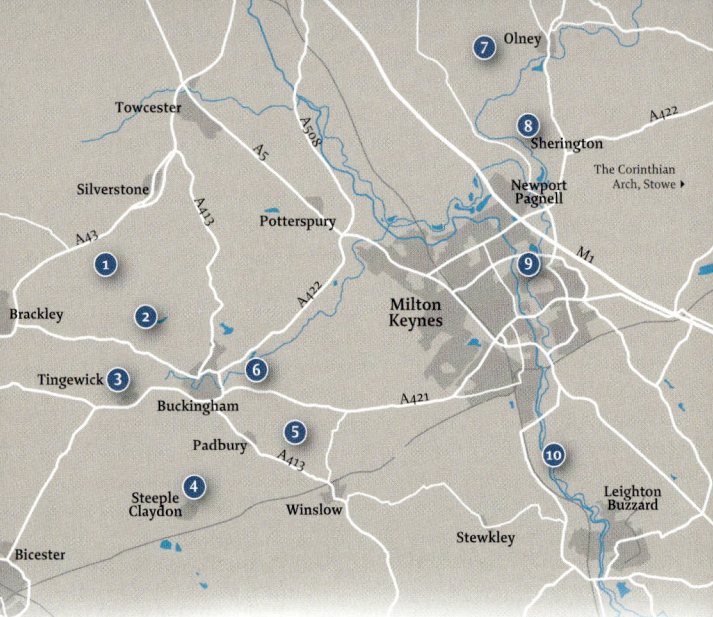

This section covers the northernmost part of Buckinghamshire, where the River Great Ouse flows eastwards from its source in Northamptonshire past Buckingham and then loops northwards around Milton Keynes before heading into Bedfordshire.

Buckingham is the main town in the west of this part of the county and it was the original county town. The land here is characterised by farmland and scattered villages such as Biddlesden and Tingewick. The parkland of Stowe and its famous gardens have been landscaped out of this rolling countryside and provide a stark contrast.

To the south and east of Buckingham groups of villages like the Claydons and the Horwoods are clustered in between streams feeding the Great Ouse and make for some longer walking routes.

The new town of Milton Keynes now dominates the north of the historic county, where Willen Lake along with its parkland is one of the city's areas providing both access to green spaces and a haven for wildlife.

To the north, across the M1 motorway, lies the old market town of Olney and a string of villages on either side of the Great Ouse, while to the south the Grand Union Canal passes below villages such as the Brickhills situated high on a ridge near the border with Bedfordshire.

North Buckinghamshire

1. **Biddlesden** 10
   Hike around some medieval border country once farmed by monks

2. **Stowe Gardens** 12
   Explore the temples, grottoes and monuments in one of England's most majestic planned landscapes

3. **Tingewick and Water Stratford** 14
   Visit two charming villages with interesting churches on either side of the River Great Ouse

4. **Steeple Claydon and Hillesden** 16
   Take in an impressive Gothic 'cathedral' on this pleasant round

5. **Great Horwood and Adstock** 18
   Stroll along bridleways, lanes and field paths on this undulating circuit

6. **Thornborough and the Ouse Valley** 20
   Keep an eye out for the subtle signs of early settlements on this tour

7. **Weston Underwood and Ravenstone** 22
   Enjoy the sights that inspired the poetic works of William Cowper

8. **Sherington and Tyringham** 24
   Shadow the River Great Ouse on this lovely parkland loop

9. **Willen Lake** 26
   Loop around this new town lake, enjoying a variety of sights on the way

10. **Great Brickhill** 28
    Cruise along the towpath of the tranquil Grand Union Canal

Biddlesden

Distance 7km **Time** 1 hour 45
Terrain mostly level lanes, tracks and paths over fields and through patches of woodland **Maps** OS Explorer 192 & 207
Access no public transport to the start

Biddlesden is an estate hamlet and lies in the northwestern part of Buckinghamshire on the border with Northamptonshire. In medieval times Biddlesden, along with the village of Syresham just across the county border, was more populous than it is today. It stood at the northern limit of the ancient royal forest of Whittlewood and for 400 years the surrounding land was worked by the monks of a Cistercian abbey founded here in the 12th century.

After its dissolution under Henry VIII, the last physical remains of the abbey disappeared with the construction of Biddlesden House and Park in the early part of the 18th century. However, the names of Abbey Farm Cottage, Abbey House and Whitfield Wood, passed along the route, are a reminder of this almost forgotten history.

Walk up the lane past the entrance gates to Biddlesden Park House, round the bend past Abbey Farm Cottages and down across the dip. Off to the right here, part of the lake to Biddlesden House is visible. Just beyond the dip, turn left onto the footpath along the driveway towards Abbey House and, after 200m, fork right across two fields to Whitfield Wood. The route passes along the woodland ride through the trees to a gate back into fields. Bear a little to the right and continue across three more fields to a junction with the track from Woodgreen Farm, which carries a bridleway.

The route turns left along the track over the field and heads past Three Parks

◀ In fields near Abbey House, Biddlesden

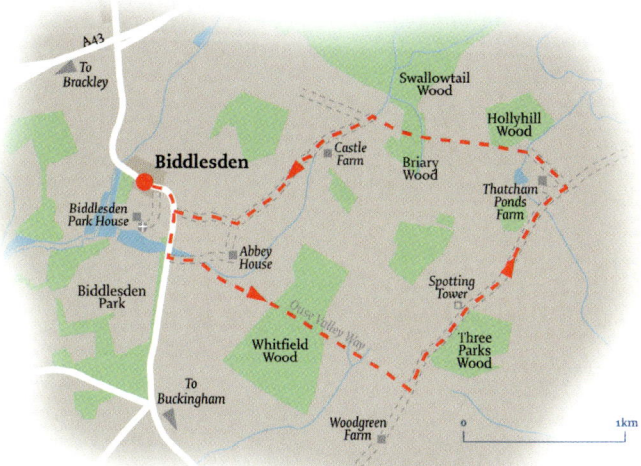

Wood. At the end of the wood there is an unusual brick tower with steps on the outside. This is a former quadrant tower for a bombing range located in the fields here during the Second World War. Continue along the field-edge track and down across the dip by the buildings of Thatcham Ponds Farm. Head up the rise to a track and bridleway junction at the top of the field in front of a house and gate. The route turns left here with the track along the top edge of the field above the farm buildings. At the second gate, fork left across two small fields past a house to gates at the far corner by Hollyhill Wood. Go through the small wooden gate between the two field gates, head along the side of the wood and then follow the left edge of the field beyond to Briary Wood.

The bridleway continues through the wood along the left edge of the marshy break in the trees (if overgrown you can make your way through the trees on the left). It then crosses the field beyond to a path junction. Turn left here and follow the grassy track between trees and hedges to a stone barn and some ruins, all that now remains of Castle Farm. A little beyond, the bridleway bends to the right through a gate. It then heads along the edges of two fields and through a patch of woodland to reach the lane again at Abbey Farm Cottages. A right turn here will take you back along the outward route to the start.

Stowe Gardens

Distance **6km** Time **1 hour 30**
Terrain **parkland tracks and field paths**
Map **OS Explorer 192** Access **no public transport to the start**

Many of the leading designers and architects of the 18th and 19th centuries contributed to the formation of Stowe Gardens, which are made up of grassland, trees, lakes, temples, grottoes and monuments. The aim was to create an ideal park which encapsulated and celebrated the quintessential forms of English countryside and culture. At the centre of the park is Stowe House, one of England's grandest mansions which, along with its surrounding buildings, is occupied by Stowe School. Managed by the National Trust, there is a fee for entry to Stowe Gardens for non-members but parking is free.

The walk starts from the National Trust car park for Stowe Gardens by its visitor centre at New Inn, which has a café and toilets and is located just north of the village of Chackmore.

Walk back along the car park access road and head past the Corinthian Arch, the grandiose main entrance to Stowe House. Fork right onto the footpath along the estate track signed for New Park and Home Farm. The track heads gently down the parkland and across the dip with Upper Copper Bottom Lake on the right. Continue up the track, which soon bends right and passes above Oxford Water and its classical bridge to the junction by the two Boycott Pavilions. The western pavilion was occupied by the garden designer Lancelot 'Capability' Brown while designing parts of the park.

The route turns right here and follows

◀ Lord Cobham's Pillar

the straight tree-lined driveway, which carries a bridleway, gently uphill and over the rise with increasingly good views off left. On the right you can look across Stowe School's playing fields to its neoclassical frontage. Continue past the school to a path junction at the right bend, where a path leads off left to Wolfe's Obelisk. This monument commemorates Major-General James Wolfe, who died capturing Quebec from the French in 1759.

The route bends right here with the driveway and heads down past the octagonal Fane of Pastoral Poetry into the dip. Fork right and follow the permissive path (waymarked with pink arrows) up the track beside railings and over the rise, from where there is a view across to Lord Cobham's Pillar. This is Lady Cobham's memorial to her husband, who owned the estate in the first part of the 18th century and was responsible for the considerable redesign and expansion of the park during this period. The permissive path doglegs to the left here off the track and continues ahead down the field edge to a gate by a lodge house. Off to the left you can see the Bourbon Tower, a former gamekeeper's house which stands at the highest point of the park.

The permissive path continues down the field beyond, across a small stream and then over three more fields. In the third field you pass the Temple of Friendship, now in ruins since being damaged by fire in the 19th century. At the far end of the field you'll find a ticket booth by the entrance to Stowe Gardens on the right. To return to the start, turn left and follow Bell Gate Drive gently back up the hill, where signs direct you back to the visitor centre and the start.

Tingewick and Water Stratford

Distance 5.75km **Time** 1 hour 30
Terrain lanes and field paths
Map OS Explorer 192 **Access** bus to Tingewick from Brackley, Buckingham and Banbury

This undulating circuit takes you between the villages of Tingewick and Water Stratford which lie either side of the valley of the River Great Ouse. This long river has its source just to the west near Brackley and meanders its way eastwards through Buckinghamshire on its journey across the country to The Wash near King's Lynn.

The walk starts from the eastern end of Main Street in Tingewick at the junction with Church Lane. Head up Church Lane towards the Church of St Mary Magdalene and a little below it look out for a footpath off left. Inside the church there is a 17th-century Faceless Clock and an unusual brass memorial to the Revd Erasmus Williams, who died in 1608.

The footpath heads along a walled walkway and then bends right to pass through a tunnel of hedges to reach a gate into fields. Follow the footpath northwards along the right edge of the first field, cross the second field and then head along a fenced section to the left of a house. The footpath then crosses the corner of a field before heading to the left through a spinney. Follow the field edge beyond and then bear half-right down the next field to Water Stratford Road near the bridge over the River Great Ouse. The name Stratford gives the clue that the modern road follows the line of a Roman road, the one from Alchester, near Bicester.

TINGEWICK AND WATER STRATFORD

◀ South doorway of St Giles Church, Water Stratford

Turn right over the bridge and head up the road into the village of Water Stratford, where you pass St Giles Church, which dates from Norman times. There is an exquisite carved tympanum over the south doorway and on the outer face of the west wall is an unusual tablet to Rector John Mason, a 17th-century composer of hymns. Continue up the pavement through the village and at the top end, just past The Manor, look out for the footpath off right over a stile into fields.

Head along the edge of the first field and across a track below a bungalow and farm buildings. Continue down the field beyond and over a footbridge in the third. Bear a little left up the fourth field towards a large black poplar tree and cross the stile beside it to reach a path junction. The route takes the right fork and heads eastwards over four more fields. Head gently down parallel to the fence in the first field and then the River Great Ouse in the second. Climb to the left of a barn in the third field and head down the edge of the fourth.

The route now turns right and heads over a long narrow field towards the embankment of the dismantled Buckingham and Brackley Junction Railway. Climb the steps up over the embankment, head across the field beyond and turn right along the edge of the next field towards Tingewick Mill. Near the end of the field the footpath bears left to a stile and footbridge by Tingewick Mill Weir. Once across, bear left and walk past the front of the former cornmill. A mill stood here for more than 1000 years and, until it was diverted in the 1960s, the River Great Ouse used to run right past the mill house. Evidence of a Roman villa has also been unearthed nearby. The final part of the route heads up the house's driveway and then follows Church Lane for just over 1km gently uphill and back down past the church into Tingewick.

Steeple Claydon and Hillesden

Distance 6.75km **Time** 1 hour 45
Terrain mostly paths and tracks over fields
Map OS Explorer 192 **Access** bus to Steeple Claydon from Aylesbury, Buckingham and Bicester

The name Claydon means 'Clay Hill' and Steeple refers to the steep hill around which the village is built, rather than to the steeple of St Michael's Church. The church is located on the eastern edge of the village and has a broach steeple, which was only added to the church tower in the 19th century. Along the route you pass Hillesden Church and House, site of a desperate siege during the English Civil War.

The walk starts from the western end of Steeple Claydon at the junction of West Street and North End Road. Go down North End Road to the bend and take the fenced footpath off left between houses to a gate into fields. Head across the first field and, in the second, turn right past a brick pumping station. Follow the field edge and cross two footbridges, the second one taking you over Padbury Brook. The footpath heads across the field beyond, then zigzags right, then left, and follows field edges as it rises gently up to Church-hill Farm.

Bend right up past the farm buildings to a track junction, bear right along the field-edge farm track and continue along the lane to Hillesden Church. This impressive church is known as The Cathedral of the Fields and is said to have inspired the church-architect Sir George Gilbert Scott's love of Gothic architecture. A panel at the edge of the churchyard explains the

◀ Hillesden Church

history of the hamlet of Hillesden, including events during the Civil War, and the local Denton family, whose grand memorials are inside the church.

The onward route turns right past the church onto the Cross Bucks Way and heads through the gateposts along the tree-lined driveway to Hillesden House. Continue down past its entrance to a gate onto the avenue which stretches out straight ahead. After just under 1.5km, at a gate at the end of the avenue, the Cross Bucks Way turns left along a field edge to a junction with a bridleway. It then turns right through trees to reach a path junction at King's Bridge. Turn right with the bridleway across the footbridge over Padbury Brook and after just under 100m look out for a footpath off right into fields, signed with a disc for the Bernwood Jubilee Way.

This waymarked route bears left over the first field and along its right edge for 50m. It then crosses a footbridge and bears half-left over a second field. Head up a third field (aim to the right of the line of telegraph poles to the gap in the hedge at the top) and cross a fourth. A little way in from the far corner of this field the footpath forks. Take the left fork to stay on the Bernwood Jubilee Way, which heads across a small ditch and then between a fence and hedge, climbing steadily up the side of two fields to reach North End Road on the edge of Steeple Claydon. The route now leaves the Bernwood Jubilee Way, doglegs right across the road and down Mitchinson Street along a walkway past houses. At the end, continue ahead on the walkway past the recreation ground and along Meadoway to West Street, where a right turn takes you back to the start.

Great Horwood and Adstock

Distance 9.5km **Time** 2 hours 30
Terrain lanes and paths over fields
Map OS Explorer 192 **Access** bus to Great Horwood from Aylesbury and Buckingham

The walk starts from the village of Great Horwood, whose attractive brick and tile cottages stand on a small ridge above fields criss-crossed by streams in the northern part of the Vale of Aylesbury. The first part of the village's name comes from the Old English word *horrh*, meaning 'muddy'. It's a reminder that the underlying soil hereabouts is clay and this walk is best attempted in dry conditions.

From St James' Church in Great Horwood walk along the High Street on the route of the North Bucks Way and bend left into Winslow Road past The Swan Inn. The route heads downhill along the pavement and then the road for 200m, where a little care is needed, to a footpath fingerpost showing the way off right through a gate into fields. From here the route to Adstock crosses a series of 10 fields, some of which can be muddy and waterlogged in wet conditions. Head diagonally left across the first field to the far corner by a brook. Keep ahead parallel with the brook past the path junction where the North Bucks Way leaves to the left and continue WSW along the edges of the next three fields.

Continue into the fifth field and bear right to pass between some fenced stands of solar panels. Cross a track and carry on to the far side of the field. You now cross a footbridge and go over two more fields before climbing gently uphill and veering a little westwards over three further fields. At the end of the 10th field, pass into a small wood and follow the footpath

◂ The churchyard and cottages in Adstock

up past a brick pumping station to the top of Scotts Lane and the junction with Main Street in Adstock. Turn right here to reach the crossroads in the centre of the village, just down from the Church of St Cecilia and The Old Thatched Inn.

At the crossroads the onward route turns right down East Street to the junction with West Street. Turn right and follow the no-through road past the houses at Greenfields, round the left bend and up the hill. In 800m, the lane becomes a bridleway and continues northwards along the track past the houses and buildings of Adstockfields at the top of the rise. After another 100m, where the track leads into a field on the right, keep ahead with the bridleway and follow it along the edges of four fields, where you head down across a dip and up to Pilch Farm.

Continue past the farm and its modern buildings, which now house various businesses, and keep on along the surfaced entrance road to Pilch Lane. The final section of the walk turns right along this pleasant and undulating lane between fields, where initially there are wide grass verges. After 3km continue ahead along Singleborough Lane to reach the junction of Winslow Road and the High Street in Great Horwood.

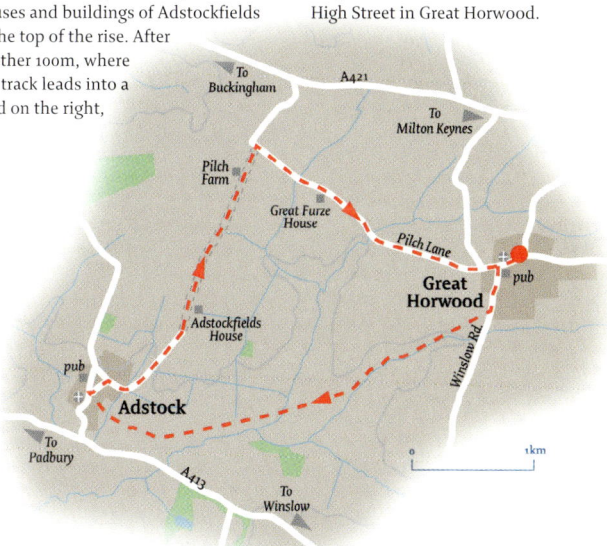

Thornborough and the Ouse Valley

Distance 9km **Time** 2 hours 30
Terrain lanes, fields and towpath of a disused canal. The River Great Ouse is prone to flooding **Map** OS Explorer 192
Access no public transport to the start

The walk starts from the centre of the pretty village of Thornborough, where the Thorn Brook runs past its greens and old stone houses. The River Great Ouse flows to its north and meets Padbury Brook (known locally as The Twins) before flowing past Thornborough Mill, which is passed along the route.

From The Green walk down to The Square and bear right along Back Street past the ford. Continue over the rise and down past the cricket ground to the junction with Lower End. The route turns right here up the lane and round the bend to a crosspaths below the top of the rise.

Turn left onto the footpath along the farm track over three fields. Where the track bends left to farm buildings, keep ahead alongside a small wood and then turn right down its edge into fields. Follow the footpath down the field edge and then turn left down the next field towards the stone buildings at Thornborough Mill.

The route heads past the front of the 18th-century Mill House and then bears left over the sluice and weir across the River Great Ouse. Turn left here through the trees to a gate into fields. The route now heads along the field-edge footpath beside the river and then bears right through a willow spinney to a gate. Cross the two fields beyond and head into a plantation of poplar trees to the disused Grand Union Canal, Buckingham Arm.

You now turn left and follow the waymarked Ouse Valley Way along the

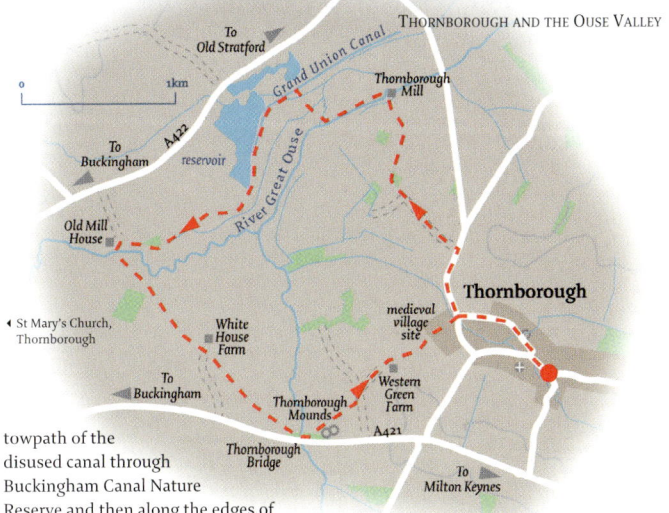

◀ St Mary's Church, Thornborough

towpath of the disused canal through Buckingham Canal Nature Reserve and then along the edges of four fields, following the line of the former canal to the track by Old Mill House. Cross the track, turn left off the Ouse Valley Way and head over the field beyond to a footbridge back over the River Great Ouse, on the far side of which is a footpath junction.

The route forks left here and heads southeastwards over five fields, climbing steadily uphill to the entrance track to White House Farm. Continue in the same direction over the top of the large field beyond and then descend over two more fields to old Thornborough Bridge. This six-arched bridge dates from the 14th century and is the only one of its kind in Buckinghamshire. Evidence of much earlier settlement has been found here, including a pre-Roman trackway, a Roman temple site and two Roman burial barrows, known as the Thornborough Mounds.

Turn left over the bridge across Padbury Brook (the modern bridge carrying the A421 is just to the right) and then turn left back into fields. The footpath bears half-right up past Thornborough Mounds to a gate onto a track at the top of the field. Dogleg left, then right up the entrance track to Western Green Farm. After just 50m go through the gate on the left and follow the field edge, parallel with the driveway, up to a gate to the left of the house. The dips and mounds in the field ahead are part of what remain of the deserted medieval village site of Thornborough. The final part of the route heads half-right down this field to the far side, turns left down one more field and passes along a hedged section down to Hatchet Leys Lane. Walk along the lane to the junction with Lower End and then retrace your steps along Back Street.

Weston Underwood and Ravenstone

Distance 6.5km (incl two short detours)
Time 1 hour 45 Terrain lanes, tracks and fields Map OS Explorer 207
Access no public transport to the start

Still standing on the High Street in Weston Underwood is the house called Cowpers Lodge, named after the 18th-century poet William Cowper. He became one of the best known poets of the day for his translations of Homer's *Iliad* and *Odyssey* and for his long poem *The Task*. In this he explores the beauty of nature and the simplicity of country life and is seen as a forerunner of the Romantic poets. In nearby Olney another of his former homes now houses the Cowper and Newton Museum. Cowper thought Weston Underwood the loveliest village in England and often walked to his nearby Alcove to seek inspiration.

From the High Street near the northern end of Weston Underwood, head up Wood Lane. This pleasant lane rises gently past cottages and between fields before dipping down to a junction with a bridleway. You can detour off right here for 150m down round the right bend and up to a gate on the right to Cowper's Alcove. The onward route forks left off the lane along the hedged bridleway track which rises gently and heads over a rise. After just under 1km you pass the track off right to Woodlands. Continue ahead for another 150m and, where the track bends right, look out for the bridleway off left through the hedge.

The bridleway follows the twisting field edge and then heads down through a strip of scrubby woodland to reach the top of the lane called North End. Turn left along this hedged lane to the edge of

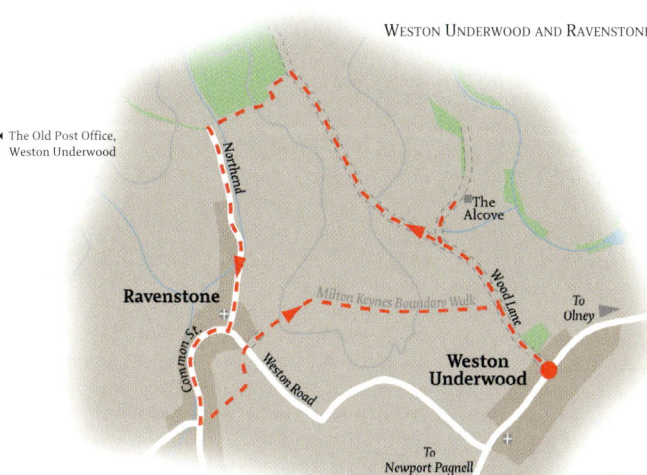

◀ The Old Post Office, Weston Underwood

Ravenstone and continue up past the cemetery and almshouses to the road junction by the Church of All Saints. Inside is a grandiose marble memorial to Heneage Finch who was Lord Chancellor to Charles II in 1675. He built the nearby almshouses and is buried, along with many family members, in the crypt below the monument. The monument does not record that it was Finch who had argued for the hanging of the poet John Milton on the grounds that Milton had been Latin secretary to Oliver Cromwell.

The onward route turns right along Common Street past Abbey Way and the entrance to Abbey House, reminders that this was the site of an Augustinian priory. At the bend you can detour off right down the lane towards Parkfield Farm, from where you can see the outline of the former priory's fish ponds. Continue round the bend down through the village past the pretty cottages and houses, the village hall and the recreation ground to the junction with the road to Stoke Goldington. Take the footpath off left here up between houses and then up the edge of the field beyond. Bend left into a second field and cross its top corner to a gate onto Weston Road opposite the houses of The Close.

The route crosses over the road and heads past the houses to a gate into fields. You now follow the waymarked footpath gently up over a series of five fields – follow the edge of the first two fields and in the second, after 100m, fork right across it. At the footpath junction on the far side of the third field, take the left fork through a gate. Dogleg right along the edge of the fourth field and left down the fifth to reach Wood Lane by a bungalow. Turn right back down Wood Lane to the start.

Sherington and Tyringham

Distance 8.5km (incl short detour)
Time 2 hours 15 **Terrain** lanes, tracks and field-edge paths **Map** OS Explorer 207
Access bus from Olney and Milton Keynes stops on High Street at the green on the western edge of Sherington

Sherington is a substantial village based around a square of lanes joining its medieval 'ends'. The village is unusual in having the only church in the country that is dedicated to St Laud, a 6th-century French bishop. The parish of Tyringham lies further up the Ouse Valley, but there is no village here – just a church, a bridge and an historic mansion surrounded by parkland fields.

The walk starts from Church End on the eastern side of Sherington near St Laud's Church. From Church Road head up Gun Lane past the White Hart hotel. Continue up the lane for another 500m past houses and out of the village to the junction with High Street. Cross over and take the footpath a little to the right into fields. The footpath follows the field edge up over the rise, down across a dip and up to a bridleway junction at a crosstrack.

The route turns left and follows the bridleway along the right field edge. After 150m make sure you fork right with the bridleway which heads into the neighbouring field and continues in the same direction on the other side of the hedge. Near the end of this long field the bridleway is funnelled down a hedged section. It then turns sharp right up beside a hedge, over the rise and down to Hill Plantation. Turn left and keep along the bridleway through the woodland. At the far end the bridleway turns left along

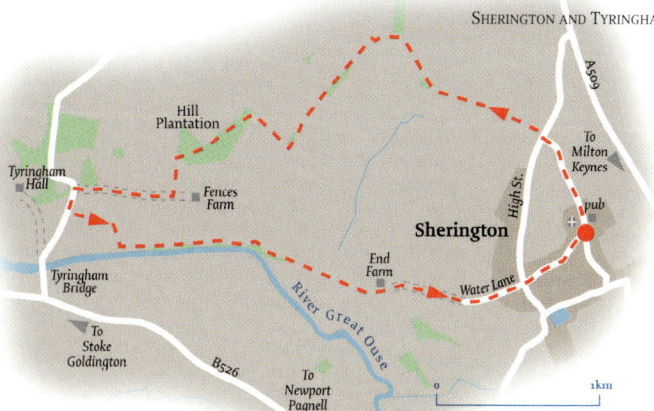

a field edge and down through a couple of gates onto Fences Lane near Fences Farm. Turn right and follow the lane for 600m past Far View Lodge and then a couple of semi-detached farmhouses to the road in Tyringham.

Turn left down the road through the parkland of Tyringham Hall and after 150m look out for the bridleway off left along the Ouse Valley Way, which is followed back to Sherington. You can make a short detour further down the road to Tyringham Church, which overlooks the River Great Ouse and contains various memorials to the Tyringham family. A little further on is Tyringham Bridge from where you can get a glimpse of Tyringham Hall. These were built to the designs of the renowned architect Sir John Soane in the 1790s for William Praed, who had married into the Tyringham family.

The Ouse Valley Way bridleway heads eastwards along field edges for the next 2km. In the third field the path drops to the right down to the River Great Ouse and follows its bank, which is lined with some magnificent black poplars. Beyond, the bridleway takes you along more field edges to reach End Farm. You now walk along the farm's driveway and up Water Lane to the junction with High Street at the western edge of Sherington.

Cross over and head along Church Road past The Knoll, the village green. A panel on the village pump records an unusual meeting here in 1935. The rival universities of Oxford and Cambridge had chosen Sherington as a suitable place midway between the two cities to 'bury the hatchet'. In putting aside their differences they hoped to unite against the growing dominance of newer universities. The ceremony was re-enacted in 1995 as part of the parish council centenary celebrations. Keep on up Church Road for the final 500m to return to the junction with Gun Lane by St Laud's Church.

◀ Tyringham Bridge over the River Great Ouse

Willen Lake

Distance 5km (incl short detour)
Time 1 hour 15 **Terrain** lakeside paths and woodland **Map** OS Explorer 192
Access bus from Milton Keynes town centre to Woolstone Roundabout West on H6 Childs Way, 200m from the start

On 23 January 1967 tens of thousands of acres of North Buckinghamshire were designated as the site for a new city to be called Milton Keynes. This 'new town' was designed to incorporate a number of existing villages. One of these was the village of Willen and it was here that two lakes were constructed in the 1970s as balancing lakes to help prevent flooding. The lakeside has been developed over the years and among the leisure facilities there are a number of landmarks, including the Observation Wheel, the Peace Pagoda and the Medicine Wheel.

The walk starts from the western side of South Willen Lake at car park A and completes a clockwise circuit of both North and South Willen Lakes. It's also possible to start from car park B by the Observation Wheel. From car park A head towards the South Lake and turn left past the lakeside buildings and slipways towards the 36m-high Observation Wheel. The surfaced Redway path takes you past a promontory on the right, which houses Willen Lake Watersports Centre and The Willen Lake Café. Keep on along the Redway path past car park B to the northern edge of the lake and, where the path forks, keep left and pass under H5 Portway to reach North Willen Lake.

Follow the path along its western edge, where you soon pass The Circle of Hearts Medicine Wheel. This sculpture consists of two concentric circles of stone

◀ The South Lake at Willen

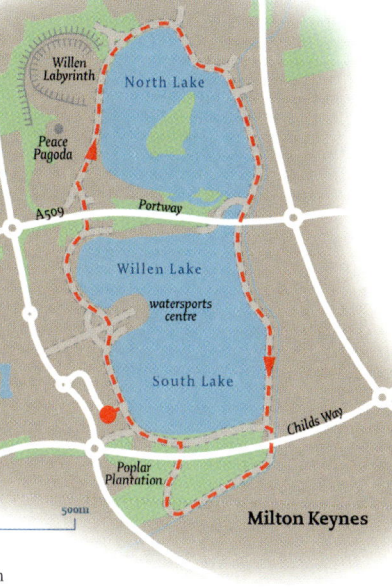

and was inspired by the legends of the North American Hopi Nation. At the path junction beyond turn right and pass below the Peace Pagoda, where you can detour left up steps to visit this stupa created in 1980 by the monks and nuns of the Nipponzan Myohoji spiritual movement.

Continuing, you pass *Souls in Love*, a white marble sculpture by Frederic Chevarin, and then the Labyrinth, a turf maze with an oak tree at its centre. At this point follow the lakeside path to the right of the surfaced Redway and keep on along the lake's northern shore past Willen Hospice, formerly Manor Farm. At the path junction 100m beyond you can detour off left for 200m into Willen village to see the 17th-century Willen Church, built almost entirely of brick to a design by Robert Hooke, a colleague of Sir Christopher Wren.

The path now passes along the lake's eastern shore, where you cross over the flood control defences. Continue along the raised bank to the path junction at the southern end of the lake.

Here the route bears left to complete the circuit of the South Lake. A shorter option would be to take the path ahead which passes between the lakes and returns to the start along the South Lake's northern shore.

The onward route passes back under the H5 Portway and along the South Lake's eastern shore, which is often lined with people fishing. On reaching the far end of the lake you can either bear right along the lakeside path back to the start or keep ahead to pass under H6 Childs Way and follow the path beside the River Ouzel through the Poplar Plantation. After 500m at the bridge over the river turn right and follow the path through the middle of the plantation and back under Childs Way. At the lakeside path turn left past the Treetop adventure park and then fork right to return to the start.

Great Brickhill

Distance 6.5km **Time** 1 hour 45
Terrain lanes, fields and canal towpath
Map OS Explorer 192 **Access** bus to Great
Brickhill from Leighton Buzzard and
Bletchley (very limited service)

Great Brickhill lies to the southeast of Milton Keynes near the county border with Bedfordshire and is one of three villages bearing the name, the other two being Little Brickhill and Bow Brickhill.

This village has been known as Much Brickhill and Brickhill Magna and has a long history stretching back to at least Roman times. The Roman road of Watling Street is not far away and remains of Roman cremation have been found in the southern part of the village at Holts Green. This contrasting circuit takes you from the high ground on which the village stands down fields to the Grand Union Canal in the Ouzel Valley to the west of the village.

From the centre of Great Brickhill at the crossroads by The Three Trees, walk along Lower Way in the direction of Bletchley and Milton Keynes for 600m to St Mary's Church. Inside are monuments to the Duncombe family, who first came to the village in the 16th century and lived in the old Manor House until it was demolished in the 20th century. The route turns left down Church Lane and just before the bend, opposite Orchard House, forks right through a gate onto the public footpath. Head down through a second gate and along the right side of the field beyond, parallel with the estate wall, to its bottom right corner. There are good views westwards here over the Oxfordshire Plain.

Follow the path down through two more gates and then along the edge of woodland with a field on the left. The

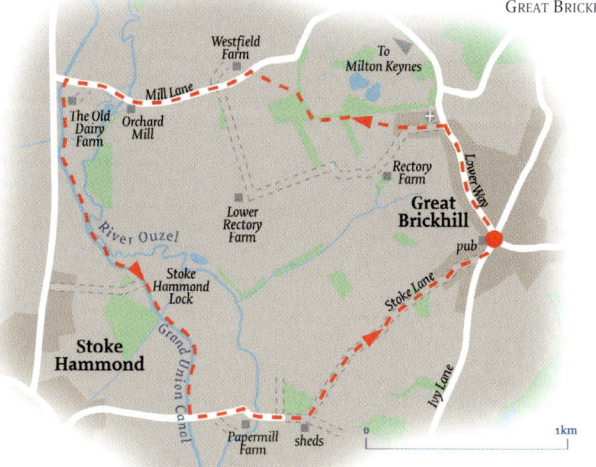

path soon bends right with the fence along the lower edge of the woodland to reach a field. The right of way heads diagonally across to the far corner, but if recently ploughed or crops block the way, follow the left-hand field edges. At the far side go through the hedge onto Mill Lane, opposite Westfield Farm. Turn left down the lane, cross the River Ouzel by Orchard Mill and continue past The Old Dairy Farm to the bridge over the Grand Union Canal.

The route turns left before the bridge, down steps onto the towpath, and heads southwards along it for just under 2km. The canal was originally called the Grand Junction Canal and when it was completed in 1799 it significantly reduced the distance for transporting goods by canal between Birmingham and London. The pleasant surfaced path, which also carries National Cyclepath 6, winds its way beside the canal and passes under the bridge at Stoke Hammond Lock. Continue for another 700m to the next bridge, which carries the lane from Stoke Hammond. Just before the bridge turn left with the cyclepath to the lane and then turn left along it.

The lane heads between fields and then bends right past Papermill Farm, where it becomes a bridleway track. Continue ahead over the River Ouzel and up the track to a bridleway junction by some farm sheds. The route forks left here and follows the pleasant hedged and tree-lined bridleway path. The gradient gradually steepens as you climb back up the hill and after just under 1km you reach the bottom of Stoke Lane. Head up this lane past Broomhill House to the junction with Ivy Lane in Great Brickhill and turn left past the attractive brick and timber Cromwell Cottages, in origin a 16th-century tithe barn, to return to the start.

◀ Stoke Hammond Lock on the Grand Union Canal

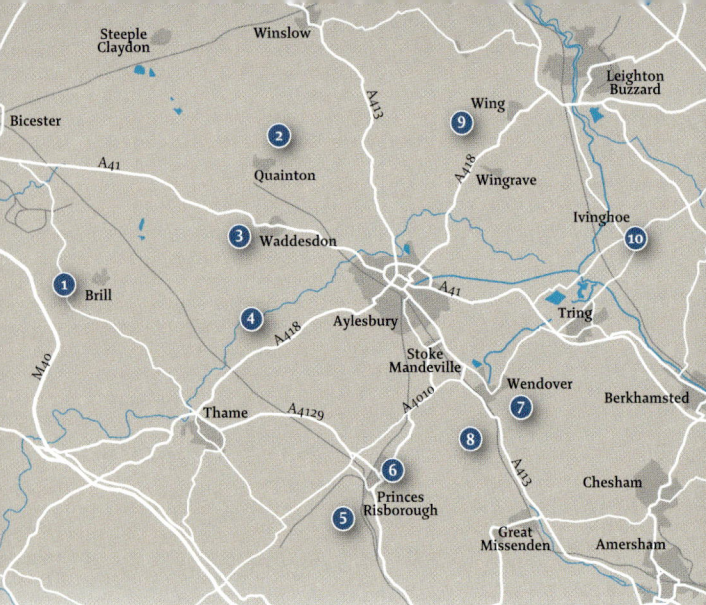

This section covers the ground from the Vale of Aylesbury to the northern escarpment of the Chilterns. In the west, walks from the villages of Brill and Quainton, both famous for their windmills, give long views into Oxfordshire. The estate village of Waddesdon is the setting-off point for a circuit of the parkland and fields surrounding its French château-like manor. In contrast is the walk to the south between the ancient villages of Nether Winchendon and Cuddington which face each other on opposite banks of the River Thame.

Aylesbury is the county town and its conurbation dominates the surrounding plain with its network of connecting major roads. The ground to its south runs flat right up to the northern edge of the Chilterns, where towns such as Princes Risborough and a line of villages are strung out along the foot of the escarpment. Here are some more demanding walks which follow sections of the ancient Icknield Way and climb the steep slopes up to the even more ancient Ridgeway. The high points of Whiteleaf Hill, Coombe Hill and Ivinghoe Beacon all give spectacular views, while the open-access wooded heights above the small historic town of Wendover are a magnet for all types of outdoor enthusiasts.

Looking south from Ivinghoe Beacon to Steps Hill ▶

Mid Buckinghamshire

1. **Brill and Boarstall** — 32
   Start out from a landmark windmill and pass an historic gatehouse

2. **Quainton Hill** — 34
   Climb out of the village for fine views over the Vale of Aylesbury

3. **Waddesdon and Westcott** — 36
   Enjoy a circuit around a magnificent château and landscaped gardens

4. **Cuddington and Nether Winchendon** — 38
   Take in two pretty villages sitting on opposite sides of the River Thame

5. **Bledlow and Lodge Hill** — 40
   Follow well-worn waymarked paths for far-reaching views

6. **Princes Risborough and Whiteleaf Hill** — 42
   View an ancient chalk hill carving on this hike from the market town

7. **Wendover Woods** — 44
   Explore the woodland trails in this family-friendly forest

8. **Coombe Hill and Dunsmore** — 46
   Ascend to the highest point in the Chiltern Hills for a panoramic view

9. **Wing, Aston Abbotts and Cublington** — 48
   Tour a trio of characterful villages set in peaceful countryside

10. **Ivinghoe Beacon** — 50
    Reach the northern end of the Ridgeway on this classic climb

Brill and Boarstall

Distance 7.5km **Time** 2 hours
Terrain lanes, tracks and field paths
Map OS Explorer 180 **Access** bus to Brill from Aylesbury and Princes Risborough (limited service)

The walk starts from the village of Brill which stands high on a hill overlooking the plain of mid-Oxfordshire. The village's name combines two Celtic and Saxon words for hill and its most well-known landmark is its photogenic 17th-century windmill. This stands prominently on the common to the west of the village and has been much refurbished over the last 250 years. Halfway along the route is another prominent landmark. Boarstall Tower is a three-storey gatehouse and was originally part of a larger fortified medieval manor house which was demolished in 1778.

From the High Street walk down Windmill Street to Brill Common where you'll find Brill Windmill. Bear left down South Hills beside the common to a six-way track junction. The dips and holes which pock-mark the common here are former claypits. From late medieval to Victorian times the clay extracted here was used to make bricks, tile and pots. Continue ahead and after 75m turn right onto a public footpath over a stile into fields on the route of the waymarked Bernwood Jubilee Way, which is followed to Boarstall Wood. The route descends three fields, crosses a stream and heads across the field beyond and through a spinney to a lane.

Turn left along the lane past Ox House, go round the right bend and continue along the lane. There are wide grass verges to avoid any traffic and the view

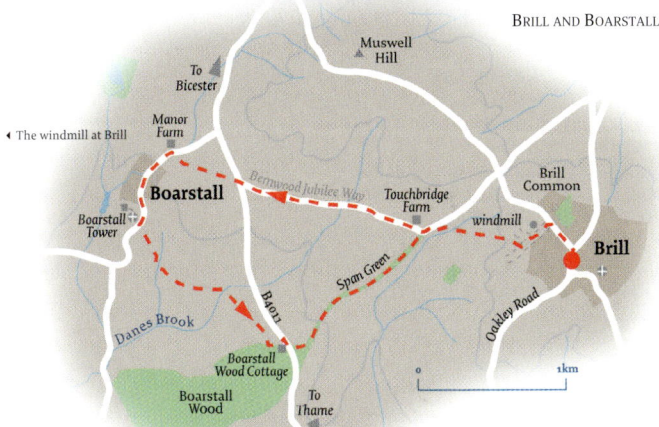

◀ The windmill at Brill

soon opens out to the communications mast on Boars Hill, west of Oxford. After just over 1km, at the junction with the B4011, cross over and take the footpath ahead through a spinney. Continue along the edges of two fields to the lane opposite Manor Farm on the northern edge of Boarstall.

Turn left along the lane into Boarstall past Tower Farm, where Boarstall Tower is just visible through the trees, and continue to St James' Church. Past the south door at the far end of the churchyard is a wrought-iron gate through which you can glimpse Boarstall Tower's lawn, the former moat of the once grand manor. The site is now managed by the National Trust.

Opposite the church just past The School House, the return route turns left back into fields and continues along the Bernwood Jubilee Way. Head diagonally across the first field to its far corner, through a spinney and along the left edge of the second field. The route now passes through a patch of woodland and crosses Danes Brook. You now bear right over two more fields to a footpath junction by Boarstall Wood, 100m to the right of Boarstall Wood Cottage.

At this point leave the Bernwood Jubilee Way and turn left along the field edge to the cottage, which stands on the B4011. Turn right and just past the cottage cross the road (a little care is needed) onto a footpath into scrubby woodland. Head through the woodland to a junction with a wide grassy track, known as Span Green. The route turns left along this old track for a little over 1km. Initially you pass through woodland, where it can be muddy and wet, and then along a hedged section between fields to reach the bend in the lane near Ox House. Head up the lane onto the outward route past the house and, a little beyond, turn right back up fields into Brill.

Quainton Hill

Distance 9km **Time** 2 hours 30
Terrain fields, lanes and farm tracks
Map OS Explorer 192 **Access** bus to Quainton from Aylesbury

Quainton was the birthplace of the antiquarian George Lipscomb. He was born at Magpie Cottage by The Green in 1773 and pursued a medical career, publishing many volumes on both medicine and local history, but his major work was *The History and Antiquities of the County of Buckingham*. A plaque in the Church of the Holy Cross and St Mary commemorates his endeavour and the fact that he died in poverty in London in 1846. Among the other memorials in the church are the marble monuments to the local Dormer family and a wall monument to Richard Brett, one of the translators of the Authorised Bible.

The walk starts from The Green in Quainton, above which stands the village's restored windmill, a tower mill dating from 1830. Walk up to the top of The Green past the medieval cross and bear left past Magpie Cottage along Upper Street. After just over 100m take the footpath off right up beside a house, called The Vine, and along a hedged passageway to a gate into fields. The route follows the North Bucks Way, which climbs the grassy slopes of the hill's southwest spur up past the Jubilee Beacon, from where there are long views over the Vale of Aylesbury. On a very clear day you can see the Shropshire Hills. The North Bucks Way then heads NNE up over three fields to reach a stile in a hedge west of the hill's communications mast. Cross the stile and bend right up beside the field edge to a crosspaths with a

bridleway at the top of the broad crest of Quainton Hill just north of the mast. Turn left across the field to a gate, beyond which the bridleway splits.

The route leaves the North Bucks Way here and takes the left fork (ahead) along an indistinct path – an ash tree and a line of hawthorn trees show the way – after which the right of way bends a little left down to a gate. Beyond, the bridleway heads down the hill's northwest spur and, after 250m, drops left down to the fence just above Hogshaw Hill Farm. Here, the bridleway bends right to reach a gate onto the farm's driveway. Bear right and follow the driveway downhill to the lane which runs along the north side of the hill.

Now turning right, the route follows this pleasant lane between fields with good views up the northern side of Quainton Hill. After just over 1.5km you reach the junction with Carters Lane by Stonemill Farm. Turn right up Carters Lane, which passes between fields to the east of the hill. Carry on over the rise and gently downhill for just under 1km to a house on the left opposite the farm track to Denham Hill Farm.

Turn right along the track, which carries a bridleway, past farm buildings and up over two fields to Denham Hill Farm. The route turns left here with the bridleway down the farm's driveway and over a stream to the entrance to Ladymead Farm. Turn right along the field-edge track past the farm buildings of Denham Lodge. A little further on follow the track over the cattle grid into the field on the right to reach a track junction. Turn left down the field-edge track to the junction with Church Street on the eastern edge of Quainton. A right turn takes you up to the church and round the bend past the almshouses back to The Green and the start.

◂ The Jubilee Beacon on Quainton Hill

Waddesdon and Westcott

Distance 7km **Time** 2 hours **Terrain** lanes, tracks and paths over parkland and fields **Maps** OS Explorer 181 & 180 **Access** bus to Waddesdon from Bicester and Aylesbury

This walk starts from the village of Waddesdon and follows the public rights of way around the privately-owned Waddesdon Estate. Waddesdon is an estate village and many of the buildings are painted in its signature plum colour. The Rothschild family bought the land in 1874 and on top of the hill here built a French Renaissance-style château which would not have been out of place in the Loire Valley. The route passes over the pedestrian access path to Waddesdon Manor near the start of the walk and it would be feasible to include a visit to the main house, which is now managed by the National Trust.

From the western end of the High Street by the war memorial, head down Silk Street, which carries a bridleway. Pass through the entrance gates to Waddesdon Manor and continue round the bend to the barrier. Here, fork right off the driveway with the bridleway, which heads alongside a hedge and then over the parkland. It crosses over the surfaced pedestrian access path to Waddesdon Manor and then reaches a T-junction of estate driveways. Flanking the driveway just off to the right you can see four allegorical statues entitled America, Europa, Asia and Africa.

At the junction continue to follow the bridleway along the driveway ahead, which climbs gently uphill and winds its way along the south side of Windmill Hill. After crossing the second cattle grid make sure you take the track off left with the

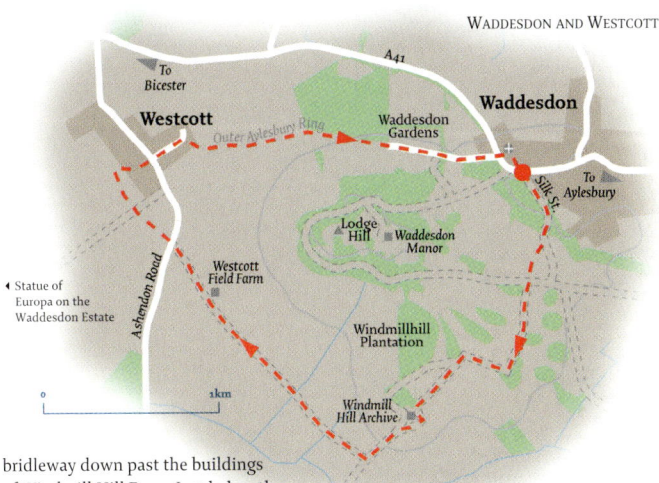

bridleway down past the buildings of Windmill Hill Farm. Just below the farmhouse the bridleway turns right and passes along a track below the modern buildings to a junction. Here, turn left down past an estate cottage to the bridleway junction at the valley floor.

The route now turns right and follows the field-edge track northwestwards for a little over 1.5km, with views off right to the towers and turrets of Waddesdon Manor and Lodge Hill. Continue past Westcott Field Farm and then Westcott Cricket Club to reach Ashenden Road. Here, you join the waymarked Outer Aylesbury Ring path, which is followed back to Waddesdon. The route crosses the road and continues ahead into fields. Cross the first field, head over a disused entrance road and follow the right edge in the second field. At the far end turn sharp right through a thicket into the third field. The line of the path bears a little to the right and then heads past houses (a little over to the left) to a gate onto the High Street in Westcott.

Cross over and continue along Lower Green to the bend. The route forks right with the Outer Aylesbury Ring path back into fields and heads along the left edge of the first field. After 100m make sure you fork left through the smaller of two gates. Cross two more fields and then walk along a grassy track between high hedges to the walls of Waddesdon Gardens. Continue along the surfaced track with the high wall on your right to the estate road junction at its far end. Keep ahead up Queen Street past The Dairy and continue to the High Street at the western edge of Waddesdon. Cross the road and go along the lane to the Church of St Michael and All Angels. Head past the south door and bear right down through the churchyard to rejoin the High Street near the start.

Cuddington and Nether Winchendon

Distance 6km **Time** 1 hour 30
Terrain lanes, bridleways, and paths over riverside fields, liable to flooding and muddy in winter **Map** OS Explorer 181
Access bus to Cuddington from Aylesbury (limited service)

Enjoy a short but varied walk between two pretty villages which lie on opposite sides of the River Thame and whose contrasting churches are both dedicated to St Nicholas.

From The Green in Cuddington head down Upper Church Street past Cuddington Stores and the stone, timber and brick Bernard Hall to the church. The interior was significantly renovated in the 1850s by the architect GE Street and there are some fine examples of Victorian stained glass in the windows. Continue round the bend past Tyringham Hall, which dates from the 17th century, and head along Lower Church Street to its grassy green. Bear left here and continue along Frog Lane to the bend by a thatched house called Spicketts.

The route forks left here onto a bridleway which heads along a track. This soon narrows and becomes tree-lined, making for pleasant walking for the next 1km to reach the rear entrance to Ridgebarn Farm. Keep ahead through the trees for another 100m and then take the footpath off left over a stile and down the left field-edge. At the bottom of the field continue round to the right and bear left across the bridge over the River Thame. Continue across the field beyond alongside a ditch with some willow trees. On the far side cross the stile and then turn immediately left over a second stile.

The route now makes its way west and southwest along field edges below Mainshill Farm towards Old Mill – in the

CUDDINGTON AND NETHER WINCHENDON

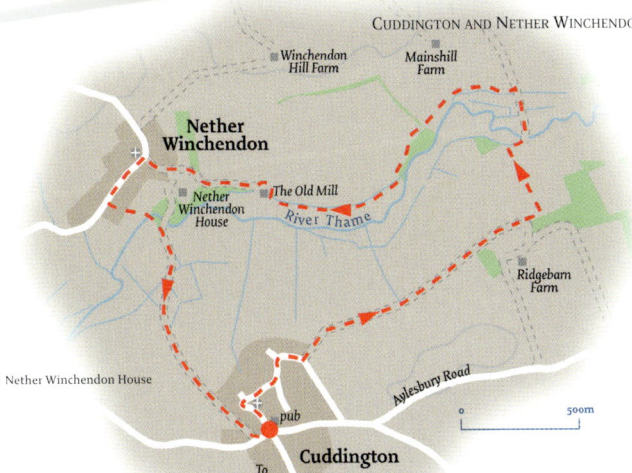

◀ Nether Winchendon House

second field, where the ground steepens, cross left over a double stile and bear half-right across the third field. At the far end the footpath doglegs through a gate on the right into a fourth field and continues ahead on the right of the fence. After 250m the right of way then turns left back over a stile in the fence and heads briefly along the edge of woodland. Go through the gate into the fifth field and turn right along its edge to its far end. At Old Mill bear right past its corrugated barn and then turn left to reach the now-renovated house's driveway.

Follow the footpath along the driveway and up the lane beside the wall of Nether Winchendon House, in origin a much restored medieval manor house and home to the Tyringham, Bernard and Spencer family since Tudor times. Continue past its entrance gates to the junction and small green with its Victorian pillar box in the centre of Nether Winchendon. Opposite is St Nicholas' Church which is mostly unrestored and still has its box pews in its simple interior. The name Winchendon is an unusual one and comes from the old English word for 'lapwing'. These now endangered crested plovers with their black and white appearance and 'peewit' call can still be spotted in the surrounding fields.

The route forks left at the junction along the wide lane through the village and after 250m, just before a red telephone box, turns left onto the footpath past the brick and timbered Langlands. From here, continue to the bridge across the River Thame and keep ahead along the field edge beyond to reach the track at the rear of Nether Winchendon House. Follow this track for the final 1km, climbing gently back up the hill into Cuddington.

MID BUCKINGHAMSHIRE

Bledlow and Lodge Hill

Distance 8km **Time** 2 hours 15 **Terrain** tracks, lanes and field paths with one steep ascent **Map** OS Explorer 181 **Access** bus to Bledlow from Princes Risborough (very limited service)

The village of Bledlow is set on a spur of the Chilterns southwest of Princes Risborough near the county border with Oxfordshire. The village is an ideal setting-off point for the high ground of Lodge Hill and the route follows the well-waymarked Chiltern Way and the Ridgeway path.

The walk starts from Church End where parking is available in the small parish council parking area by Manor Farm. Walk along Church End to the western end of the village and fork left up past The Lions of Bledlow pub. The route turns left here up the byway, signed for the Ridgeway. At the bend in the track continue ahead, climbing steadily uphill to a track junction with the Icknield Way and the waymarked Ridgeway path, which is followed for the walk's middle section.

Dogleg to the left along the track and then bear right with the Ridgeway path into fields. The route heads down across a dip and along two field edges to Wigan's Lane. Cross over and continue ahead over two more fields to a fenced section which takes you up into woodland on the northwest spur of Lodge Hill. Follow the path steeply up through the trees and along the top of the hill, from which there are some long views northwards. The Ridgeway path descends the hill's eastern slope to a bridleway junction and then winds its way along field edges to Lee Road. Cross the road, head down the driveway past Longwood Farm and then continue between fields to a gate. The Ridgeway path now doglegs left, then

◀ Near Wigan's Lane approaching Lodge Hill

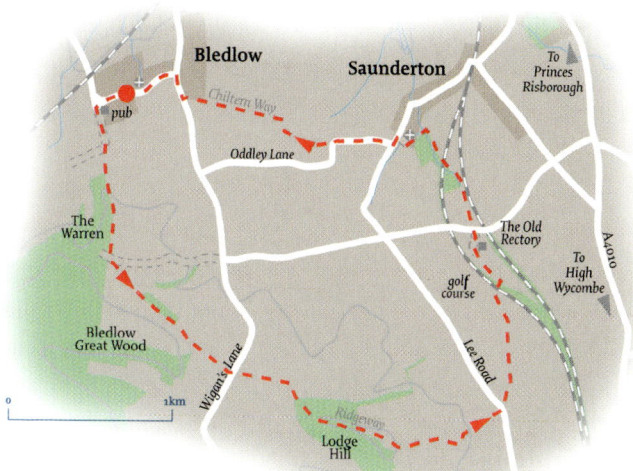

immediately right down between the fairways of Princes Risborough Golf Course and across the railway line into the field beyond.

Here, leave the Ridgeway path, which continues ahead, and turn left onto the waymarked Chiltern Way, which is followed back to Bledlow. Head up the field and down past The Old Rectory along its driveway to the lane at the bottom. The Chiltern Way crosses this lane, the Upper Icknield Way, and continues along the edge of a long field. Before the end of the field go left over a stile in the hedge and recross the railway. The Chiltern Way continues along the left edge of the field beyond. After 200m turn left down across a stream and continue up past Saunderton Church to the lane. The route now turns right along the lane to the junction with Bledlow Road. Turn left along the road for 50m to the next junction and take Oddley Lane off right, signed for Chinnor and Bledlow.

Follow this narrow lane for just under 400m to a sharp left bend and take the footpath ahead into fields. Head over two fields and into the trees on the far side to reach a junction with a byway. The Chiltern Way doglegs right for 50m along the byway, then left onto a bridleway, which crosses a large field to Bledlow Ridge Road on the edge of Bledlow. Turn right along the road, then take the first left back along Church End to the start.

Mid Buckinghamshire

Princes Risborough and Whiteleaf Hill

Distance 5.25km **Time** 1 hour 45 **Terrain** tracks and paths over fields and through woodland, with some steep sections **Map** OS Explorer 181 **Access** bus to Princes Risborough from Aylesbury and High Wycombe

Situated in a gap in the Chiltern Hills, Princes Risborough takes its name from Edward, the Black Prince, who was its landowner in the 14th century, and from the old English words *hrisenan beorgas* meaning brush-covered hill. This walk climbs the steep hill immediately above the town which is known as Brush Hill, now a local nature reserve, and then heads over the wooded top of Whiteleaf hill.

From Market Square with its brick Market House in Princes Risborough, walk along to the end of the High Street, dogleg left along Horns Lane and right onto New Road. Follow the pavement up Kop Hill past Salisbury Close and then take the next left onto Upper Icknield Way. This byway track carries the Ridgeway path which is followed to the top of Whiteleaf Hill. Follow the track for just over 300m past houses to the football ground and then make sure you fork right with the Ridgeway path off the byway onto a footpath. The Ridgeway path climbs up the right edge of a field towards Brush Hill and then heads into woodland, where the gradient steepens up steps to a path junction. Continue ahead up more steps to the top of the wood, go through a gate and climb the steep-sided field beyond to reach a toposcope at the top and a handy bench for taking in the view.

The route carries on into the trees along the Ridgeway path, where it bends left to a gate and continues beyond through

◀ The view westwards from Whiteleaf Hill

Brush Hill Plantation. On reaching Peters Lane dogleg right, then left across the road. Ignoring paths off left and right, continue to follow the wide Ridgeway path which now goes over Whiteleaf Hill, leading gently down through the trees to a gate into a clearing. On the left is the hill's grassy viewpoint and below on the hill's western slope is Whiteleaf Cross. The cross is carved into the chalky hillside and is visible for miles around. No one knows its origins for certain but folklore attributes its creation to the Saxon king Edward the Elder, the elder son of Alfred the Great.

The onward route leaves the Ridgeway path here, which turns off right, and continues ahead onto a bridleway, dropping steeply down the hill's wooded northern slope to a path junction at the fence of Whiteleaf Reservoir. Pass the entrance gates and turn immediately left down the bridleway to Upper Icknield Way. The route turns left here and takes you up this pleasant lane past thatched cottages, old houses and The Red Lion pub to the junction with Peters Lane. Cross over and continue ahead along the tree-lined byway between fields for 800m to return to the football ground, from where you retrace your steps along the outward route back down into the town.

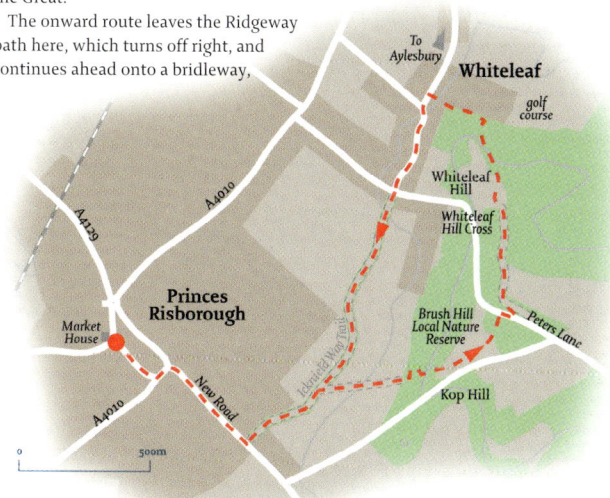

Wendover Woods

Distance 10.5km **Time** 3 hours
Terrain lanes, woodland tracks and paths
Map OS Explorer 181 **Access** bus to Wendover from Aylesbury; train to Wendover from Aylesbury and London

Wendover is an attractive market town set in a gap in the Chilterns between Coombe Hill and Boddington Hill. This walk takes you from the town centre up onto the wooded heights of Wendover Woods. In recent years these woods have become very popular with walkers, cyclists, runners and horse-riders. Many species of birds can be seen in the mixed woodland here, including firecrests and crossbills, and deep in the woods you may even bump into a Gruffalo or two.

Walk down to the bottom of Wendover High Street and just before the Clock Tower turn right onto Heron Path, signed for the Ridgeway path which is followed for the first half of the walk. Follow Heron Path between houses, past the sports ground, the Wendover Memorial Community Orchard and then Hampden Pond to Church Lane. Turn left along the lane past St Mary's Church to the junction with Hale Road.

The Ridgeway path crosses over and heads along Hogtrough Lane up to farm buildings and the entrance to Boswells. Continue ahead for another 200m to a path junction at the edge of woodland. The Ridgeway takes the left fork and now heads up through the mixed plantation of Barn Wood. The route bends eastwards, passes its high point and then bears northeastwards for just under 1.5km on an undulating path through Hale Wood to Hale Lane. A quick dogleg to the right takes you over the lane and down through the trees to a path junction. Here the Ridgeway forks left more steeply downhill

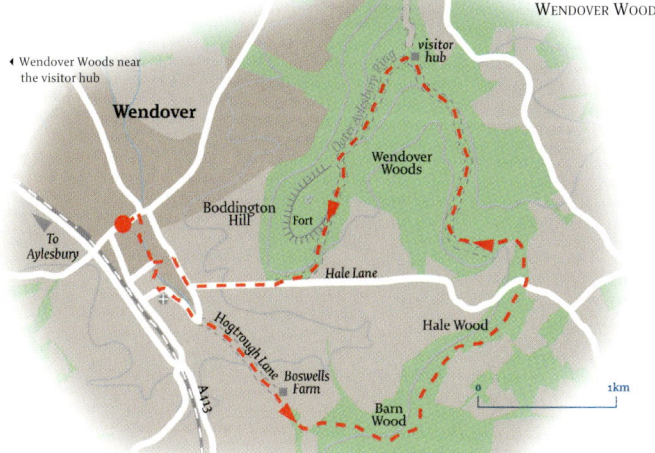

◂ Wendover Woods near the visitor hub

to a bridleway junction at the bottom of the slope.

The route leaves the Ridgeway path at this point and turns left down the sunken bridleway. After just over 100m look out for a marker post and take the well-marked footpath off right uphill for 400m to reach a track, which carries a footpath. Turn right and follow the track northwards for 800m, heading steadily up through Wendover Woods, over a rise and down to a prominent fork in the track. Keep right with the footpath, signed for the car park, for another 600m up to the top of the hill, where you'll find Wendover Woods Café and car park.

Continue a little past the café and then turn left to the Forestry Commission cabins. The route now veers southwards alongside the Go Ape centre and car park. Beyond, continue on the route of the Outer Aylesbury Ring down past a picnic area and viewpoint to a track junction at the northern end of Boddington Hillfort, which dates from the Iron Age.

Bear left here down the track and after just over 100m, at a junction, make sure you turn right with the Ring path down along the tree-covered earthworks on the hillfort's eastern edge. Beyond the hillfort continue down the track, which now descends more steeply. At the bottom of the hill reach a path junction and fork left down onto Hale Lane. Bear right down the lane for 600m to the junction with Hale Road. The final part of the walk turns right up the road, over a slight rise and down the pavement past a row of houses on the left. At the end of these houses, make sure you turn left onto a surfaced bridleway, which takes you down between gardens back to Heron Path by the Memorial Community Orchard. Turn right to retrace your steps back to the start.

Coombe Hill and Dunsmore

Distance 6km Time 1 hour 45
Terrain lanes, woodland tracks and paths
Map OS Explorer 181 Access no public transport to the start

The walk starts from the National Trust car park for Coombe Hill located at the top of Lodge Hill road above the hamlet of Coombe, near Butler's Cross, 2km to the southwest of Wendover. Coombe Hill, which is reached near the end of the walk, is the highest accessible point (260m) in the Chilterns and gives long views northwards over the Vale of Aylesbury. On top of the hill is a monument which commemorates the men of Buckinghamshire who died in the South African War (Second Boer War). It was erected in 1904 and then rebuilt in 1938 after being struck by lightning and almost completely destroyed.

Walk back out of the car park and turn left down the lane going southeastwards in the direction of Dunsmore. After 500m, just before the gateway to Upper Bacombe, take the bridleway off left into Low Scrubs, an area of woodland which for centuries was commonland. Head down across a shallow dip and up to a bridleway junction by a fence. The route turns right here, heads across the track to Upper Bacombe and continues along the fenced bridleway through the wood of High Scrubs to the edge of the small village of Dunsmore. As you come out of the trees continue along the lane past houses to the junction opposite the chapel by a small green and pond in the centre of the village.

The route turns right here, signed for Kimble and Princes Risborough, and follows the lane steeply downhill. At the

COOMBE HILL AND DUNSMORE

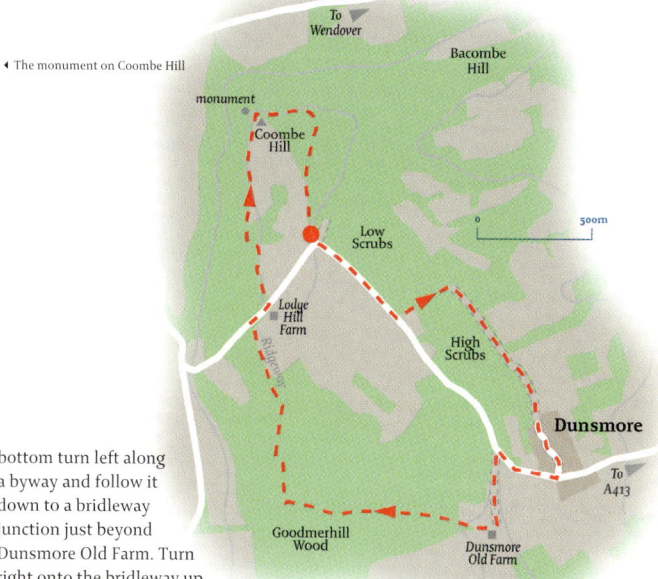

◀ The monument on Coombe Hill

bottom turn left along a byway and follow it down to a bridleway junction just beyond Dunsmore Old Farm. Turn right onto the bridleway up past the gates to Cobnut Farm and then past a house called Ashmore into woodland. Continue up through the trees for 300m to a five-way path junction. Take the footpath ahead (to the left of the bridleway) and continue up through the wood to the top of the rise and the junction with the Ridgeway path.

You now turn right and follow the Ridgeway path's frequent waymarks northwards for 800m to Lodge Hill road, where it doglegs right up the road for 100m and then turns off left through trees to reach a gate. Go through the gate and continue to follow the Ridgeway path as it makes a short dogleg down to the left out of the trees and then right into a field. Follow the top edge of the field with a grand view westwards over whale-backed Beacon Hill as you climb gently up to the monument at the top of Coombe Hill. The final part of the walk bears right at the monument off the Ridgeway path, which descends the hill's northern slope towards Wendover, and follows the obvious surfaced and level path for 800m eastwards and then southwards alongside a fence back to Lodge Hill road and the car park at the start.

Wing, Aston Abbotts and Cublington

Distance 12.5km **Time** 3 hours 15
Terrain lanes, tracks and field paths
Map OS Explorer 192 **Access** bus to Wing
from Aylesbury and Milton Keynes

Stride out on this longer walk over farmland between the villages of Wing, Aston Abbotts and Cublington.

From Church Street in Wing follow the footpath through the churchyard to the left of All Saints' Church and descend the field beyond to a gate into a second field, where the footpath splits. Take the footpath ahead up the bank and bear half-right down to a footbridge across a stream. Head gently uphill in a WSW direction over three fields and then along the edges of two more to reach a path junction. Keep ahead over another two fields to a crosspaths 150m into the second one. The route turns left across this field and then continues SSE over three more fields to a crosspaths 75m into the third one. You now turn right and head WSW once more. The footpath soon bears a little right to reach a gate and then continues up the edges of four more fields. At the end go through a gate onto a hedged track, which takes you to The Green in Aston Abbotts.

Turn right through the village past St James' Church and, just before the village limit, take the footpath off left alongside a garden to a gate on the right into fields. The route now heads in a NNW direction on a well-waymarked path over three fields and through three gates along a fenced section. Continue up three more fields to a driveway. Beyond, the footpath continues over four more fields and bears left through a gate into a fifth field near the houses of Cublington. At the end,

WING, ASTON ABBOTTS AND CUBLINGTON

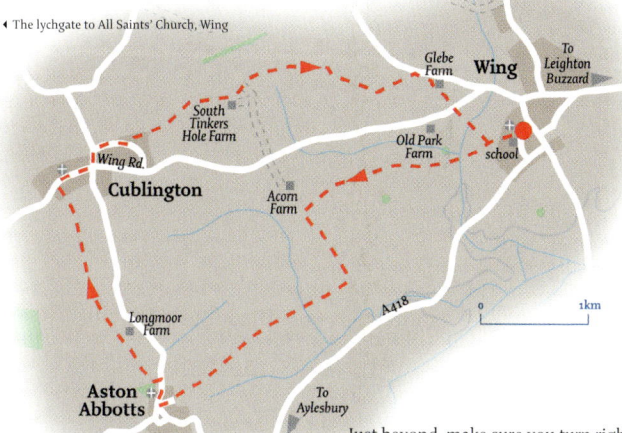

◀ The lychgate to All Saints' Church, Wing

head a little to the left to reach a fenced walkway along to Whitchurch Road.

Turn right past the church and continue along the High Street to the crossroads, where the route turns left along Stewkley Road. Pass the cricket ground and turn right along Reads Lane, on the route of the Outer Aylesbury Ring which is followed back to Wing. After 350m, by the entrance gate to Rockwell, turn left over a stile and bear right past farm sheds and along a fenced section into fields. The route now heads over two fields and then doglegs briefly right, then left along the edge of a third. Continue through a strip of scrubby woodland and along the edge of a brambly field to reach a track. Dogleg right, then left along this past South Tinkers Hole Farm and continue over a crosstrack to reach a modern house.

Just beyond, make sure you turn right off the track to a gate back into fields. Cross the first grassy field and go through a strip of scrub into the next field. Bear half-left up to a line of trees and scrub which divides this large second field. Pass along its left edge and, after 50m at the marker post, switch to the other side and continue in the same direction. At the far end bend right to a stile in the corner and head diagonally up the third field. Cut across the corner of the fourth field and turn left along the edge of the fifth. Just short of Stewkley Road, turn sharp right down the left edge of the field past Glebe Farm and head along the right edge of the next field to Cublington Road. Cross over and pass along the edge of two more fields to a footbridge. Head up the field beyond to a gate on the left and turn left through it onto the outward route back up to Wing.

Ivinghoe Beacon

Distance 7.5km **Time** 2 hours 15 **Terrain** fields and waymarked paths with one section of steep ascent
Map OS Explorer 181 **Access** bus to Ivinghoe from Leighton Buzzard, Aylesbury and Luton

This classic hill walk starts from the centre of the village of Ivinghoe and takes you up the steep slopes of Beacon Hill, known as Ivinghoe Beacon, the highest point on this section of the Chilterns.

Head along the High Street past St Mary's Church up Church Road. The church has some interesting features, among which are its carved poppy-head pew ends, so called from *poupée*, the French word for 'doll'. There is also the 15th-century Angel Ceiling which is carved with wooden figures. At the bend turn left along Vicarage Lane to the junction by The Rose and Crown pub. Turn right up Wellcroft and at the top continue past the entrance to Ivinghoe Golf Club onto the bridleway, which is followed for the next 2km. This pleasant and undulating hedged path takes you alongside the golf course and between fields to a farm track past Crabtree Farmhouse. Beyond, where the farm track bends left, keep ahead along the bridleway to reach the lane to Ivinghoe Aston.

Just before the lane take the footpath off right into fields. The route follows the left edge up the first field and then turns right down beside the fence and across the dip in the large second field. At its far end turn left and head up to the B489. Dogleg to the right along the pavement to cross the road and then head up Beacon

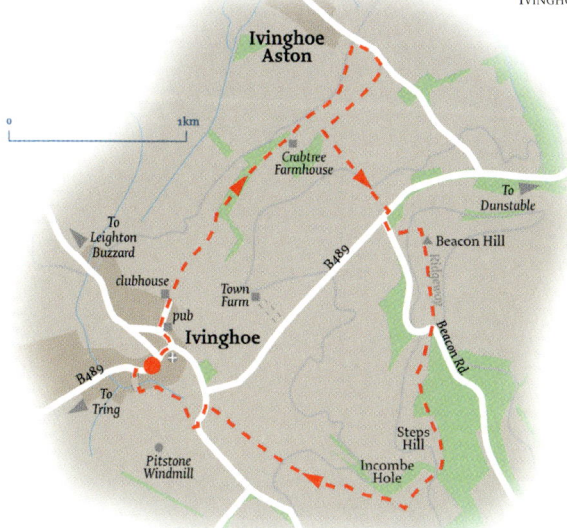

Road to the cattle grid. Take the footpath off left here up the steep western slope of Ivinghoe Beacon – you can either take the well-worn chalky path ahead or the slightly less steep but grassier path a little way to its left up past a prominent pine tree. At the top are some wide views over the Vale of Aylesbury and Oxfordshire. The hill is also the northern end of the Ridgeway path which tracks its way southwestwards along chalk escarpments for 140km to Avebury in Wiltshire.

The route heads along the waymarked Ridgeway path for just under the next 2km, down across Beacon Road and up Steps Hill – to follow the Ridgeway path after Beacon Road, fork right to a gate and then bear left uphill over the rise. As you descend, there is a good view right over the steep-sided Incombe Hole and along the line of chalk hills stretching southwestwards. Bend right with the path round the combe down to a crosspaths.

The route leaves the Ridgeway path here and turns right, signed for Ivinghoe, onto a footpath down two fields and along a fenced section to the B488. Turn left along the verge and narrow pavement and cross over a little before the bend. Go through the small parking area for Pitstone Windmill into the field beyond. The final part of the walk turns right onto a permissive path along the field edge and follows it round to the left past houses to a crosspaths. Turn right through the gate and follow Green Lane back up to the High Street, where a right turn will take you back up to the start.

◀ Above Incombe Hole

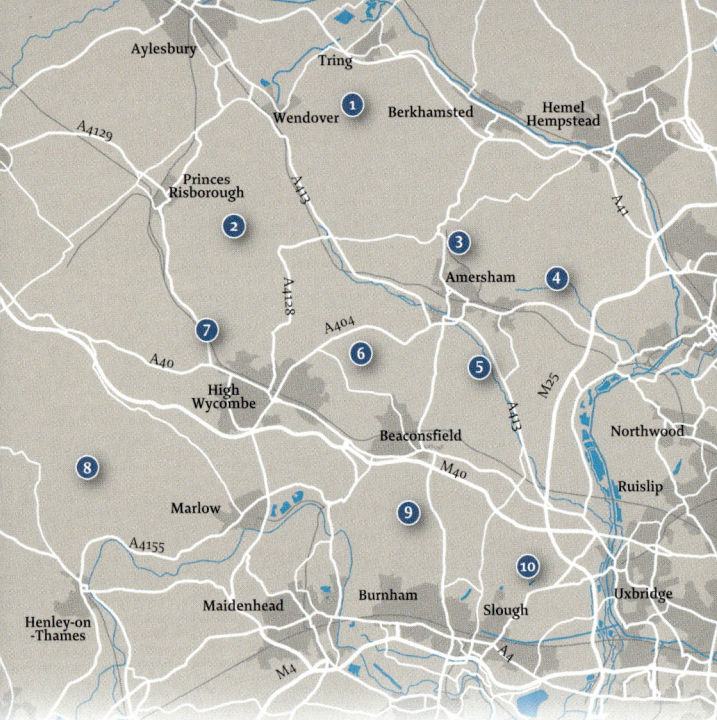

This part of Buckinghamshire is dominated by the southern slopes of the Chiltern Hills, which rise in fits and starts from the Thames Valley to their steep northern escarpment overlooking the Vale of Aylesbury. The M40 motorway cuts through the heart of these chalk hills as it speeds past the busy towns of Beaconsfield and High Wycombe.

To the north is a plateau-like patchwork of villages, commons and fields among wooded folds and small ridges. Running along its northeastern limit are the scenic valleys of the Misbourne and the Chess, one of the Chilterns' best known chalk streams.

In the southwest corner of this region lies the Hambleden Valley and the Thames-side town of Marlow, while southeastwards are the old commons of Burnham Beeches and Black Park, isolated pockets of greenery near the county border, which has moved from the natural frontier of the Thames to just north of Slough.

The village green at Chalfont St Giles ▶

South Buckinghamshire

1. **Cholesbury** — 54
   Walk among ancient earthworks and through wooded commons

2. **Great Hampden** — 56
   Loop around the ancestral home of a rebellious landowner

3. **Chesham and Tyler's Hill** — 58
   Hike up the hill from the market town before returning through valley meadows and woodland

4. **Chenies and the Chess Valley** — 60
   Set out from a charming village for a walk along the riverbank and through water meadows

5. **Chalfont St Giles** — 62
   Follow in the poet John Milton's footsteps on this easy farmland loop

6. **Winchmore Hill and Penn Wood** — 64
   Head through pleasant woodland that was once common heathland

7. **West Wycombe and Bradenham** — 66
   Take in an extravagant mausoleum and infamous caves before touring the surrounding countryside

8. **Hambleden Valley** — 68
   Climb wooded hillsides before returning through farmland

9. **Burnham Beeches and Egypt Woods** — 70
   Explore ancient woodland full of wildlife and historic interest

10. **Black Park Country Park** — 72
    Tour a sprawling former deer park frequently used as a filming location

SOUTH BUCKINGHAMSHIRE

Cholesbury

Distance 6km **Time** 1 hour 45
Terrain fields, woods and lanes
Map OS Explorer 181 **Access** bus to
Cholesbury from Chesham (limited service)

The village of Cholesbury is situated in an area of high wooded commons and upland pasture whose formation stretches back to pre-Norman times. Part of the route follows the ancient boundary earthwork of Grim's Ditch and near the start of the walk is the Iron Age Cholesbury hillfort.

The walk starts from the western end of Cholesbury Common by the village hall. Parking is possible at various points alongside the common on Cholesbury Lane and in the small parish council parking area beside the cricket ground. Take the footpath to the side of the village hall along the track and over two fields to the northern entrance to Cholesbury Camp. You can detour left or right to explore the hillfort's earthworks. This was a multivallate camp, part of a chain across the Chilterns, and it is thought to have been occupied for more than 400 years until the Romans arrived in the middle of the 1st century.

The route heads through the woodland beyond, across a field and back into woodland. Turn right along the wood's edge, dogleg left, then right across Shire Lane and descend the field edge beyond to the byway junction in woodland. The route turns left here, signed for Hastoe, and follows the pleasant byway gently uphill through the woodland. Keep on past a barrier at its northern edge out of the trees and up a hedged section to a crosspaths with the Chiltern Way.

The route turns left here onto the Chiltern Way, which is followed for the middle part of the walk, and heads along

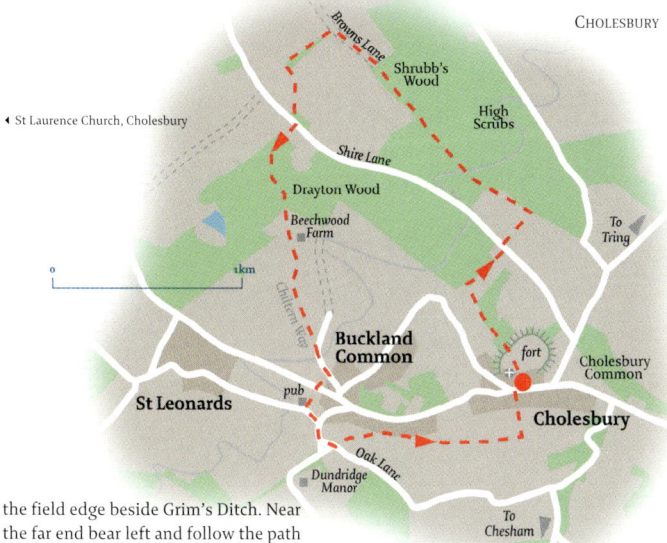

◀ St Laurence Church, Cholesbury

the field edge beside Grim's Ditch. Near the far end bear left and follow the path across the corner of the field and then through a patch of woodland to Shire Lane. The Chiltern Way continues across the lane, along a fenced section between fields and back into woodland. Just into the trees, at a fork, bear left and after another 200m, at the next fork, bear right to a gate at the edge of the wood.

You now head along a fenced section down across a dip by Beechwood Farm and up to a gate into fields. Skirt along the left edge of the first field and after just over 100m make sure you turn left through a swing gate to continue along the Chiltern Way over two more fields to Little Twye Road. Turn right down this lane into Buckland Common and after 100m take the second footpath on the right back into fields. This takes you down across Bottom Road and up to Jenkins Lane by The White Lion pub.

The route turns left along Jenkins Lane to the bend and then turns right along Oak Lane. Follow the lane round the left bend past the entrance to Dundridge Manor, where the Chiltern Way heads off right. Continue along the lane and just before the next bend look out for a footpath off left through the hedge into fields. Bear right across the corner of the first field and then head diagonally left down a couple of horse paddocks to a stile in the bottom corner. Cross the stile, walk along a fenced section between gardens and a field and then follow the field-edge path down the valley. At the end of the third field turn left for a short climb back up to Cholesbury Lane in Cholesbury, a little along from the village hall.

Great Hampden

Distance 5.5km **Time** 1 hour 30
Terrain lanes, field paths and woodland
Map OS Explorer 181 **Access** no public transport to the start

The walk starts from the village of Great Hampden and visits the John Hampden Monument before returning past Hampden House. This was the ancestral home of the Hampdens, an ancient Buckinghamshire family whose most prominent member was John Hampden, a notable Parliamentarian in the English Civil War. He had opposed Charles I and the imposition of 'Ship Money', a tax to raise money for the navy, and in 1642 he was one of five Members of Parliament the king tried to arrest for high treason. Hampden died of wounds sustained at the Battle of Chalgrove Field in Oxfordshire in 1643.

The walk starts from the road junction at the edge of Hampden Common near the Hampden Arms. Parking is available in the small parish council parking area behind the Hampden Arms or alongside the playing field on Memorial Road. This road was constructed as a memorial for those men of the village killed in the First World War, while the playing field is dedicated to those killed in the Second World War.

Head down Memorial Road past the playing field and village hall and continue down alongside wooded Hampden Common to the bend and junction. Fork left (ahead) up School Lane past houses to the next junction and a small triangle of grass. The route turns sharp left here along narrow East Lane and winds its way over a rise and down to Hampden Road. Turn right for just over 200m down the

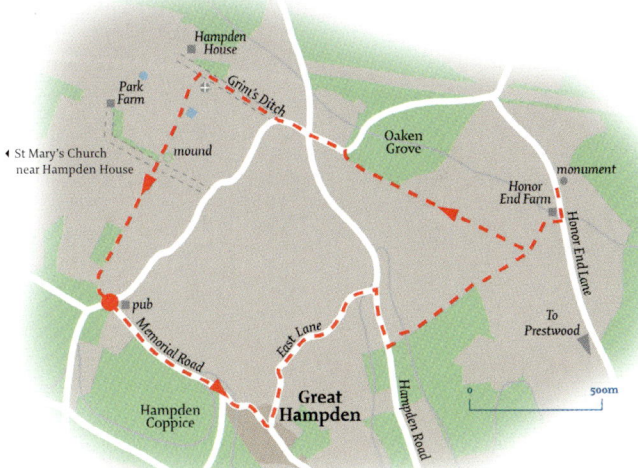

road into the trees to reach a crosspaths.

Turn left onto the footpath which heads briefly up the edge of the wood and then follows the right edge of two fields up to a crosspaths with a bridleway. At this point you can make a 600m detour out and back to the John Hampden Monument – cross the stile and continue along the fenced footpath ahead, bear right past Dairy Barn, cross Honor End Lane into the field beyond and turn immediately left onto a permissive path down the field edge for 100m to the monument (if crops block the way, you can turn left down Honor End Lane). Return the same way and turn right at the crosspaths onto the bridleway.

The bridleway heads WNW along the edges of two fields and through a wood to a road. Bear left to the crossroads with Hampden Road and keep ahead for 100m to the left bend. Continue onto the bridleway ahead which passes through a gate (press the button on the gatepost to open) and along the driveway to Hampden House and the Church of St Mary Magdalene. For a view of the private Hampden House, continue a little further along the bridleway.

The final part of the route turns left onto a footpath through the churchyard past the church to the gate opposite the south porch. Continue up the edge of the field beyond to a strip of woodland, where you can see the remains of Dane's Camp, which is thought to be the site of an early medieval motte castle. Keep ahead over a farm track, cross the next field and walk along the edge of a plantation to reach houses at the edge of Hampden Common. Bear left along their driveway to return to the start.

Chesham and Tyler's Hill

Distance 8.5km **Time** 2 hours 15
Terrain lanes, clear paths and bridleways over fields and through woodland with a final section along the waymarked Chess Valley Walk **Map** OS Explorer 181
Access bus to Chesham from High Wycombe, Amersham, Berkhamsted & Hemel Hempstead; trains to Chesham from central London

This walk climbs steeply from the market town of Chesham over the high ground of Tyler's Hill to the east and then returns along the picturesque Chess Valley.

From the clocktower walk up Chesham High Street and turn right up Station Road to Chesham Station. Turn left along The Backs and at the junction take the footpath off right up steps. Follow the walkway uphill and just before the top of the rise turn right through a gate into fields. The footpath heads up across two fields and turns left along the edge of a third. Turn right along a short hedged section to a path junction and continue ahead along the field edge, over a track by the entrance to Dungrove Farm and down the next field to a junction with a bridleway.

The route turns left here and follows the hedged and sunken bridleway for 1.25km down past Big Round Green woodland, over a path junction and gently up to Tylers Hill Road. Turn right up the narrow road – after 75m you can carry on up the edge of the field on the right – to St George's Church at the top of the lane on Tyler's Hill. Continue up the track ahead past the entrance to Cowcroft Grange and then Cowcroft Farm. Keep ahead down alongside Cowcroft Wood to a small communications mast and path junction.

Turn right onto a footpath down through the trees to a junction with a bridleway. The route turns right along the

◀ In fields just above Chesham

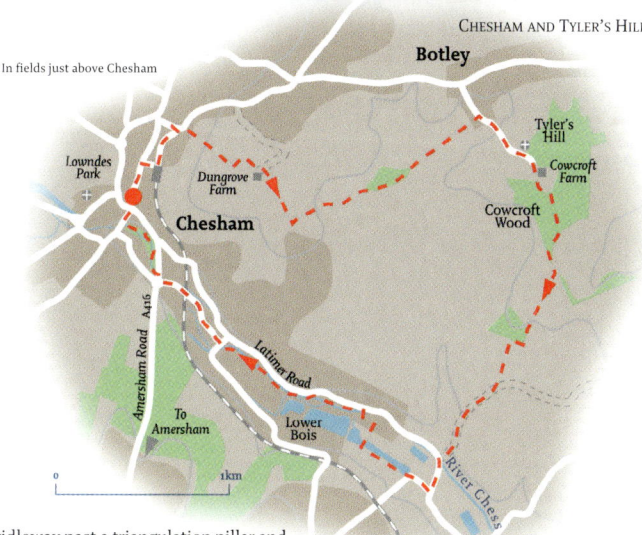

bridleway past a triangulation pillar and down out of the wood to a gate into a field. Follow the waymarks over the field past clumps of oak trees and down past a plantation to the junction with Green Lane bridleway. Dogleg right for 50m to the next junction and then take the bridleway off left. This heads down the field edge and then becomes a hedged and sunken way down to Latimer Road.

Bear left along the pavement and verge and then turn right along Holloway Lane on the route of the well-waymarked Chess Valley Walk, which is followed for the rest of the walk. At the bend keep on past Watercress Cottage and then pass along the edges of two fields. In the second field the Chess Valley Walk turns off right and zigzags its way past some works yards. It then crosses a footbridge over the River Chess and turns left along a surfaced path to the small weir at the former site of Cannon Mill.

The Chess Valley Walk switches banks and continues beside the river past boggy Chesham Moor to reach the town's playing field. At the far end, keep ahead along Moor Road past the sports centre. At the end of the terrace of houses on the right the Chess Valley Walk bears right back to the river and then left beside it. Continue along Moor Road and pass under the railway bridge to the roundabout. Bear right across Amersham Road and then take the riverside path off left through part of Meades Water Gardens to a path junction. Here, you can fork right for the station or carry on by the river to Germain Street, where a right turn will take you back to the High Street.

Chenies and the Chess Valley

Distance 5km **Time** 1 hour 15 **Terrain** lanes, fields and woodland; some sections can be muddy in wet conditions **Map** OS Explorer 172 **Access** no public transport to the start

The delightful village of Chenies stands on a small hill above the Chess Valley near the border with Hertfordshire. Its pretty cottages, flint church and brick manor house are clustered around a sloping green. In medieval times the village was known as Isenhampstead but took its current name from the Cheyne family who were lords of the manor until the 16th century. The Russell family, who later became Dukes of Bedford, then came into possession of the manor and substantially rebuilt it and the nearby St Michael's Church.

From the green, where there is some limited parking, head up the driveway of Chenies Manor House to St Michael's Church. Inside you can get a glimpse of the private Duke of Bedford chapel and tombs. At the gates to the Manor House, turn right down the walled passageway past the church tower and continue steeply down the edge of Placehouse Copse. Bear right across Latimer Road and head down the lane over the River Chess, past Dodds Mill and over the mill channel. Continue along the lane for another 100m and then bear right with the waymarked Chess Valley Walk into fields.

This heads along a bank between fields and the former water meadows. These are a rare example in the Chilterns of what used to be 'floating' water meadows. In winter these meadows were deliberately flooded by a system of sluices, streams and ditches to help improve fertility and productivity. Continue across Frogmore Meadow to a gate in the far left corner and

◀ The River Chess near Sarratt Bottom

head through the woodland beyond back into fields. Follow the field-edge path as it bends right and then left alongside the River Chess over two fields to reach a footpath and track junction near Valley Farm. The Chess Valley Walk continues ahead past the entrance to Crestyl Barn, where an information panel explains the history of Sarratt watercress beds, and along the farm track to Moor Lane. Turn right along the narrow hedged lane and at the bend keep ahead for another 500m, down past Sarratt Bottom Cottages to a crosspaths a little further on.

Here, you leave the Chess Valley Walk and turn right onto the Chiltern Way, which is followed back to Chenies. This well-waymarked route heads over the River Chess and across the water meadows, which are liable to flooding, to a path junction and gate into Turveylane Wood. The Chiltern Way then heads up through the mixed woodland for 600m and bears right through a gate. Climb the field beyond to Wyburn Wood and head along its edge. Continue along the side of the next field to reach the lane at the edge of Chenies. Cross the lane and turn right onto a footway along the grassy bank which takes you past The Red Lion and then The Bedford Arms back to the start at the green.

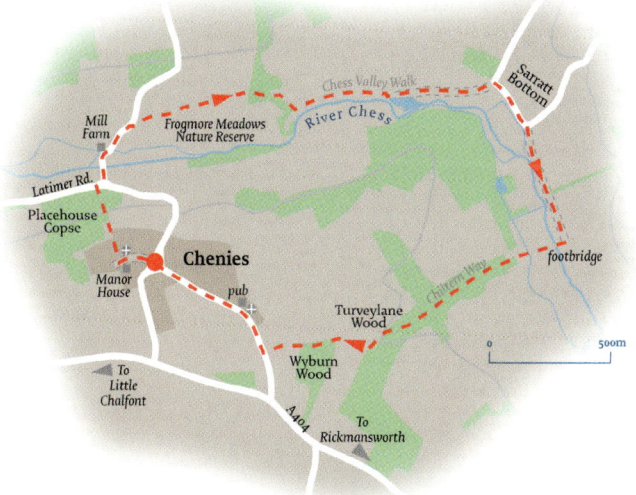

Chalfont St Giles

Distance 4km (with detour to Milton's Cottage) **Time** 1 hour **Terrain** lanes and paths through woodland and over fields **Map** OS Explorer 172 **Access** bus to Chalfont St Giles from Uxbridge, Gerrards Cross and High Wycombe

Chalfont St Giles lies in the Misbourne Valley on the edge of the Chiltern Hills. At the heart of the busy village is its green, still surrounded by local shops, cafés and businesses. Despite the traffic the place seems to belong to a previous century. Through an adjacent archway lies the Church of St Giles, patron saint of beggars and travellers, where you can see some late-medieval wall paintings. The village also has a small museum dedicated to one of the greatest English poets and political thinkers, John Milton.

John Milton's Cottage is located 250m from The Green up Deanway. The poet fled to the village during the Great Plague of 1665. He lived in the cottage for two years where he completed his epic poem *Paradise Lost* and started its sequel, *Paradise Regained*. In 1887 the inhabitants of the village established a memorial fund for the purchase of the cottage as a way of celebrating Queen Victoria's Jubilee.

From the High Street at the southern end of The Green, opposite the entrance to the parish church, head along Stratton Chase Drive on the route of the Chiltern Way. The footpath heads past houses along this no-through road, which becomes a track lined with some large chestnut trees. Continue past the last house and then a gate across the track to reach a fork. A chestnut tree in between the paths carries a waymark for The Chiltern Way. This follows the right-hand path beside a fence through the trees and then along the edge of a field to Mill Lane.

CHALFONT ST GILES

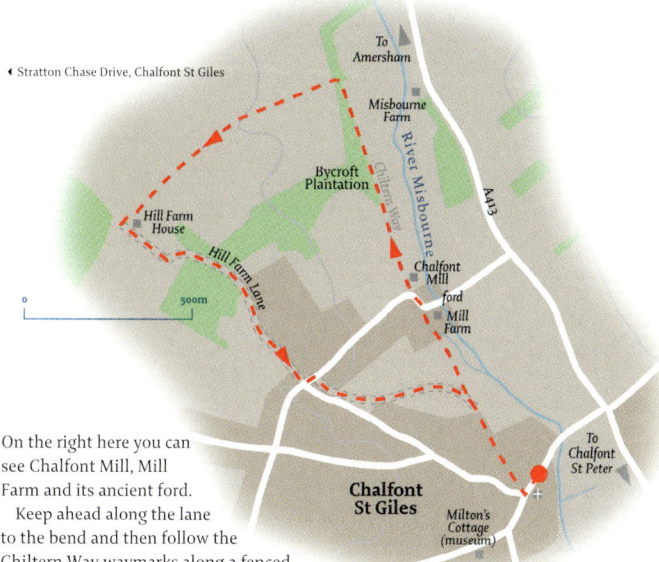

◀ Stratton Chase Drive, Chalfont St Giles

On the right here you can see Chalfont Mill, Mill Farm and its ancient ford.

Keep ahead along the lane to the bend and then follow the Chiltern Way waymarks along a fenced section between fields into Bycroft Plantation. After 400m, as you come parallel with Misbourne Farm away to the right across the field, look out for a marker-post at a footpath junction. Make sure you turn left here to stay on the Chiltern Way, which heads through a gate into fields. Follow the footpath for 700m uphill between fields, initially along a fenced section, and then up beside a hedge and fence. Continue up past Dairy Cottage and then Stable House to the junction with Hill Farm Lane.

The route now leaves the Chiltern Way, which heads off right, and turns left past the entrance to Hill Farm House.

Continue to follow the tree-lined lane as it winds its way downhill for 500m past the entrances to houses to reach a crossroads with Mill Lane. Dogleg left past a house and then right onto a permissive 'thoroughfare path' between houses into woodland. This pleasant path, originally the upper part of Stratton Chase Drive, descends gently past the bottom of gardens and is lined with large chestnut trees. After 400m, at the path junction at the bottom of the slope, bend right and rejoin the outward route along Stratton Chase Drive back to the High Street and the start.

Winchmore Hill and Penn Wood

Distance 8.25km **Time** 2 hours 15
Terrain fields, lanes and forest paths and tracks **Map** OS Explorer 172
Access bus to Winchmore Hill from Chesham, Amersham and High Wycombe

The walk starts from the village of Winchmore Hill which has a large triangular green surrounded by houses. The green is a common and was part of Wycombe Heath. This was a large area of open common land which from medieval times until the enclosures of the 1800s existed between Wycombe and Amersham. The brick-built Kiln Cottages and The Potters Arms are a reminder that the Chilterns was long a centre for the production of clay for bricks, tiles and pottery. The walk passes through Penn Wood, also once part of the heath.

Walk down to the lower (northern) end of the common to the bus stop on Whielden Lane. Cross over and take the footpath opposite up a hedged section, across a field and down along the edge of Priestlands Wood to its far end. At the path junction just into the field beyond, where the return route comes in from the left, take the middle of three paths over two fields to Penn Street. Cross over and bear right along New Road past the playing field to the bend and the Goose Pond entrance to Penn Wood.

Go through the gate onto the public footpath (the left-hand of two paths). After 100m the route turns left along a forest path, which bends round to the left, and then, a little before a gate, turns right onto a path along a forest ride lined with rhododendron bushes. Follow the forest path to a crosspaths in a shallow dip, where a memorial tree grown on the Highgrove Estate records the saving of Penn Wood from development as a golf

◀ The Chalk Track in Common Wood

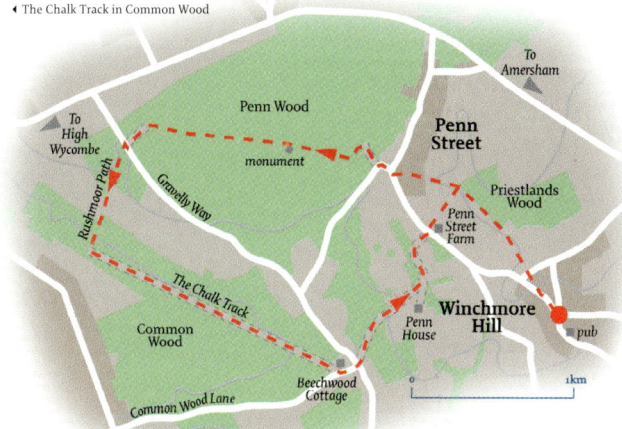

course. The path continues westwards through The Penna, the central and more open part of the wood, over two more crosspaths and then bends left downhill to the Justice Gate entrance on Gravelly Way.

Cross the road and pick up the public footpath a little to the right into Common Wood. The footpath heads down Rushmore Path through the trees and across the dip of Deadmans Dean Bottom. This gets its name from the discovery of an Anglo-Saxon grave here in the 19th century. Continue up the slope ahead and, just before the top edge of the wood, turn left onto the Chalk Track. This path, which dates from the enclosures in the mid-19th century, runs dead straight through the wood for a little over 1.5km and brings you down to The Roundabout Gate entrance at Common Wood Lane by Beechwood Cottage.

Turn left down the lane to the junction with Penn Bottom. Cross over and take the footpath opposite up into woodland to a path junction. Follow the main footpath, which forks left uphill to the top edge of the wood. Continue along a line of lime trees to the rear driveway of Penn House and follow it round to the left past Garden Cottage. Continue through the bends to the junction with Penn Street, opposite brick and flint Holly Cottages near Penn Street Farm. Cross over and take the footpath to the left of the cottages. Go through a yard and past some farm buildings to a gate into a field. Cross the field to the path junction by the corner of Priestlands Wood and turn right back onto the outward route to return to the start.

West Wycombe and Bradenham

Distance 9.5km **Time** 2 hours 45 **Terrain** paths and tracks over fields and through woodland **Map** OS Explorer 172 **Access** bus to West Wycombe from High Wycombe, Aylesbury and Oxford

The walk starts from West Wycombe, an attractive village in the care of the National Trust. The Dashwood family used to own West Wycombe Park along with the village and surrounding land. In the 18th century Sir Francis Dashwood built a mausoleum on top of the hill above the village and crowned its church with a golden globe. He also excavated the now famous caves at its foot which became a meeting place for the aristocratic members of the notorious Hellfire Club. The walk heads over West Wycombe Hill to Bradenham, another village and estate now managed by the National Trust.

From the western end of the High Street opposite the entrance to West Wycombe Park head up Chorley Road. At the Walled Garden car park turn right onto the path, signed for Hilltop and Hellfire Caves, which heads up the grassy slope and then some steps to the Dashwood Mausoleum. Pass to the right of the mausoleum and St Lawrence's Church to the gate into the car park beyond. At the far end follow the path to the left of the entrance to a track, which carries a footpath, and bear left along it gently uphill through woodland. After 1km keep right (ahead) at a fork. Follow the track over the top of the rise and continue through a gate to reach Nobles Farm.

The route turns right here onto a footpath which leads down through woodland. It then winds its way downhill along three field edges, under the railway and over the field beyond to Bradenham Road. Bear right across the road and then head up Bradenham Wood Lane past the cricket ground to St Botolph's Church. Adjacent is Bradenham Manor, whose

WEST WYCOMBE AND BRADENHAM

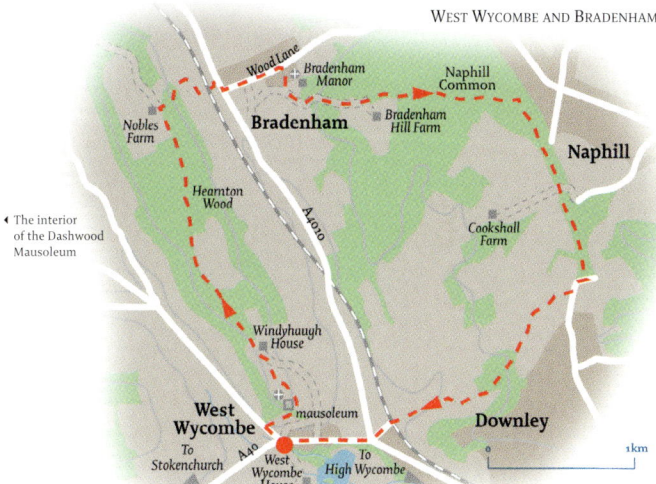

◀ The interior of the Dashwood Mausoleum

oldest part dates from Tudor times. Among its notable tenants were Isaac and Maria D'Israeli who came here in 1829 to escape the polluted air of London. The couple are buried in the crypt of the church. Their son, who was born at Bradenham, was Benjamin Disraeli, the 19th-century Prime Minister.

At the church the route turns right past the entrance to Bradenham Manor along the top of the cricket ground to a track. Bear left along the track, which carries a bridleway, climbing steeply uphill alongside the manor's wall to a path junction. Continue up beside the wall and then bend right with the track more steeply uphill past Bradenham Hill Cottages to where the track bends right for Bradenham Hill Farm. The bridleway keeps straight on here onto Naphill Common, one of the largest commons in the Chilterns. At the bridleway fork beyond, keep right (ahead) and follow the bridleway which heads eastwards over the wooded common for 1km to a bridleway junction just short of the common's eastern edge. Turn right and follow the bridleway SSE along the narrow southern spur of the common. After 700m you cross the track that leads to Cookshall Farm and then continue for another 600m past some cottages to the lane at Downley.

Turn right along the lane beside the cricket pitch and, just past the pavilion, turn right onto a bridleway. This path heads past a house and between fields. It then becomes a wooded sunken way that takes you downhill for just under 1.5km past Tilbury Wood to the top of Cookshall Lane. Turn left and pass under the railway to Bradenham Road. Cross this and follow the pavement back into West Wycombe.

Hambleden Valley

Distance 15km **Time** 4 hours 15
Terrain waymarked paths over fields and through woodland **Map** OS Explorer 171
Access no public transport to the start

The Hambleden Valley runs gently down from the higher ground around Fingest to the River Thames. It has long been an important route linking the Thames with the northern escarpment of the Chilterns, along which runs the ancient trackway of the Ridgeway. This longer walk climbs the wooded slopes on the southern edge of the Chilterns with a gentler return over fields.

From the centre of Hambleden head along the lane to the left of the church. Follow it round the bend past the north side of the churchyard and over the Hamble Brook to the junction. Turn right along the Skirmett road and after 500m, by Bell House, take the bridleway off left along Shakespeare's Way, which is waymarked at most major path junctions and is followed to Southend Common.

Follow the bridleway up between fields and then keep ahead onto a footpath leading more steeply up through woodland. Continue up beside a clearing and pass over a field back into woodland to a path junction. The Way turns right up a track and, after 200m, forks left along a path and then descends a track to a junction with a bridleway in a dip. Cross over onto the bridleway which heads steadily up through the wood and then between fields to the lane by Upper Woodend Farm. Turn right up the lane and at the junction keep ahead onto a footpath. This crosses a field and then descends through Kimble Wood to a bridleway junction in a dip. Continue ahead up through the trees and along the edge of the field beyond to a gate onto the track by Kiln Cottage. Head along the track and at the lane turn right into the

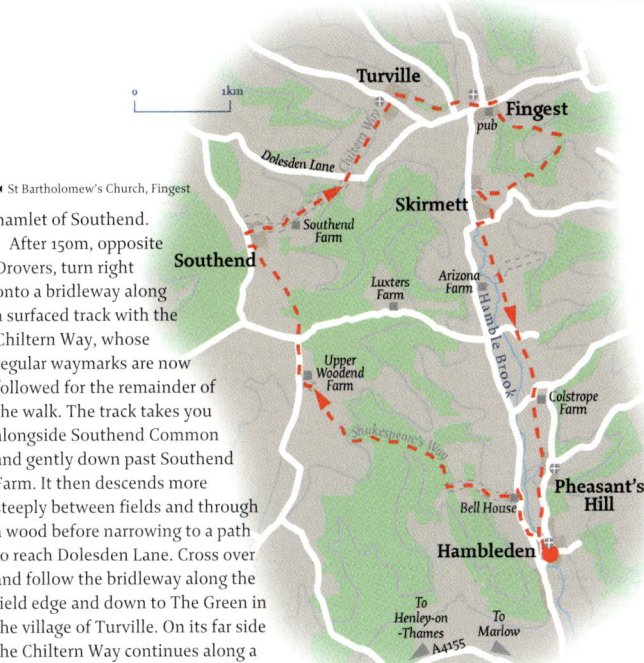

◀ St Bartholomew's Church, Fingest

hamlet of Southend.

After 150m, opposite Drovers, turn right onto a bridleway along a surfaced track with the Chiltern Way, whose regular waymarks are now followed for the remainder of the walk. The track takes you alongside Southend Common and gently down past Southend Farm. It then descends more steeply between fields and through a wood before narrowing to a path to reach Dolesden Lane. Cross over and follow the bridleway along the field edge and down to The Green in the village of Turville. On its far side the Chiltern Way continues along a track between houses, turns right up a field and passes along the top of a bank to a lane. Cross over and after 50m, at a path junction, bear right downhill to reach Fingest Lane. Turn left into Fingest past the church to The Chequers pub.

Continue for 100m along the lane and turn right into fields. The Chiltern Way now climbs steeply up the right edge of two fields. Continue up through Fingest Wood and pass over a field into Adam's Wood to reach a path junction. The Chiltern Way turns right here and makes its way downhill through the wood and then over fields to reach a small communications mast at the edge of Skirmett. Turn left over the field, then right down Shogmoor Lane and, just before the junction, go left back into fields. For the final 3.5km, the Chiltern Way takes you down the valley over fields past Arizona Farm and along a bridleway to Colstrope Farm. It then follows a footpath to Pheasant's Hill, where it passes below the houses, and from here heads over fields back to Hambleden.

Burnham Beeches and Egypt Woods

Distance 7.5km **Time** 2 hours
Terrain mostly paths and tracks through woodland and along country lanes
Map OS Explorer 172 **Access** bus from Slough and Windsor to Farnham Common stops on Beaconsfield Road (Templewood Lane stop) 500m from the start along Beeches Road and Lord Mayors Drive

Burnham Beeches has been continuously covered with woodland for thousands of years. Today it comprises extensive woodland, heath, wood pasture and wetlands. It is also famous for its many ancient pollard trees. This historic landscape came close to being built over during Victorian times but in 1879 the City of London Corporation intervened and purchased the land for the enjoyment and recreation of the public.

The walk starts from the car park on Lord Mayors Drive on the eastern edge of Burnham Beeches, accessed from Beaconsfield Road along Beeches Road. Head along the drive past the café to the crossroads at Victory Cross. Through the gate opposite is a plaque and beech tree commemorating the acquisition of Burnham Beeches. The current tree is a replacement for the one planted in 1883 by the Duke of Buckingham. Turn right along Halse Drive past a road gate and then bend left down into the dip to the junction with Victoria Drive. The route turns right and heads along Burnham Walk, whose surface was made from bricks and rubble taken from London during the Second World War. Pass over a crosspaths and continue for another 300m up to the junction with Dukes Drive opposite McAuliffe Drive. Turn right and head down the wide drive, across a dip and uphill to the northeastern limit of Burnham Beeches.

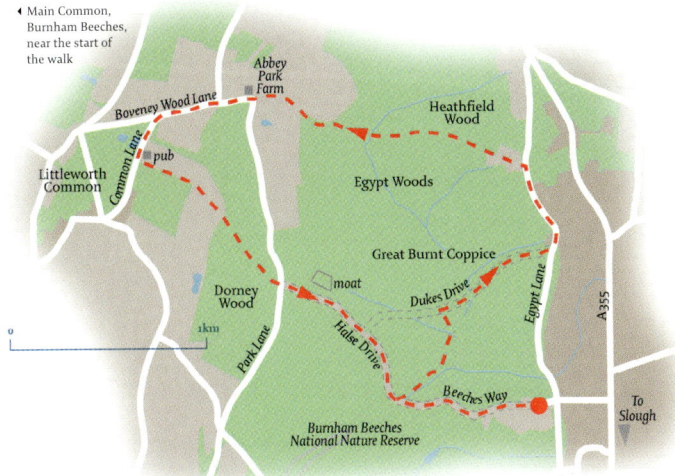

◀ Main Common, Burnham Beeches, near the start of the walk

The route forks left past cottages and then turns left along Egypt Lane. Go round the bend and head up the lane, where you can follow a path along the wood bank on the left for 400m up to the start of the entrance track to Egypt Wood Cottages. Turn left onto the public footpath along the track past the cottages and continue into Egypt Woods. After 250m the footpath starts to head down through the wood, crosses a boggy dip and then climbs up to a gate at the western edge of the wood. Head along the field edge beyond to reach Park Lane at a bend by the entrance to Abbey Park Farm. Continue westwards along Park Lane, pass the turn for Beaconsfield and keep ahead into Boveney Wood Lane. After 300m, just past the sign for Littleworth Common at the junction by Boveney Wood Farm, turn left along Common Lane to the houses by The Blackwood Arms.

Just past the pub the route turns left onto the Beeches Way along a fenced path beside a plantation and between fields down to a gate into Dorney Wood. Head up through the wood and cross Park Lane back into Burnham Beeches. Continue ahead along the Beeches Way through the trees for 250m to reach a slanted crossroads of drives and keep ahead onto Halse Drive. The final part of the walk follows Halse Drive for just over 700m through the trees and down into the dip by the junction with Victoria Drive. From here, retrace your steps back uphill to the junction with Lord Mayors Drive and the car park at the start.

Black Park Country Park

Distance 5.75km **Time** 1 hour 30
Terrain woodland tracks and lakeside path **Map** OS Explorer 172 **Access** no public transport to the start

Black Park, located to the northeast of Slough, has been managed by Buckinghamshire Council since the end of the Second World War and in 1970 it became one of the first sites in England to be designated as a country park. The land was originally part of the medieval deer park of Langley Estate, which also included what is now Langley Park to the south of Uxbridge Road, the busy A412. The park is large, stretching to over 500 acres, and comprises a variety of landscapes. The southern part of Black Park contains a large lake and is dominated by both mixed and coniferous woodland, while the northern section has areas of open heathland.

Conifers were first planted here in the 18th century, when the lake was formed by damming the stream that runs through the park. Later black pine was introduced as a timber tree, from which the park derives its name, and timber was grown and harvested commercially until the 1980s. The route passes the buildings of Pinewood Studios, the first of which were constructed in the 1930s. Many areas of the park have been used as film locations, perhaps most notably for the Hammer Horror films, a number of Bond films and the Harry Potter series.

The walk starts from the main car park for Black Park Country Park, accessed off Black Park Road. From the rear of the car park go past the modern visitor building, with its café, and at the first crosspaths turn left onto Queen's Drive, signed for the Heathland. Follow this wide forestry ride between sections of woodland for

◀ Blackpark Lake

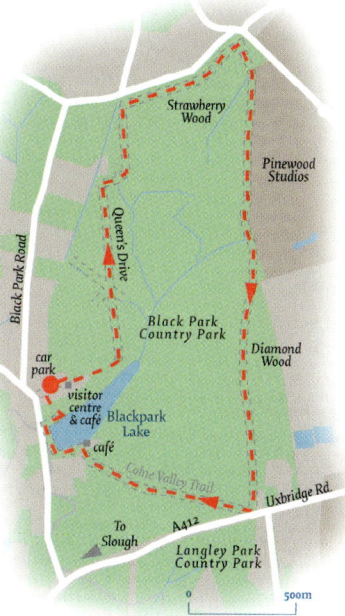

800m, over Heathland Ride at a five-way track junction and past two cattle grids to a track junction at its northern end.

The route turns right alongside a fence and at the next junction forks left to continue northwards. After 300m bend round to the right to a crosspaths. Keep ahead and follow the wide and grassy forestry ride along the northern edge of the park for the next 500m through Strawberry Wood and along Coppice Walk to a T-junction with Pinewood Ride, which carries a bridleway.

The route turns right here and follows the wide track down the park's eastern limit, where you soon pass the buildings of Pinewood Studios. At the crosspaths at the end of the buildings keep ahead and follow the forestry ride beyond past a plantation of conifers. After 500m join a gravel forest drive, which comes in obliquely on the right, and continue ahead along a section lined by the chestnut trees of Diamond Wood until you reach Uxbridge Road.

Bend right here onto the Colne Valley Trail and follow the public footpath which heads northwestwards along Rhododendron Drive. This attractive ride is lined not only with rhododendron bushes but also handsome Scots pine among the chestnut and oak trees. After 500m head over a prominent crosspaths, known as Ron Owen's Crossroads, and continue ahead for another 300m to reach the café by Blackpark Lake. The final part of the walk bears left around the southern edge of the lake and along the far side to the lake's outflow, where a path leads off left back to the car park.

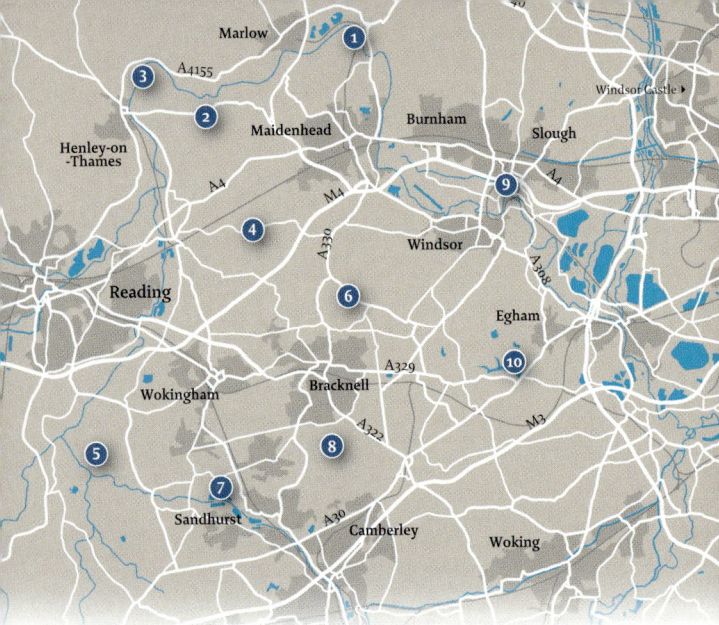

The historic county of Berkshire used to stretch northwards from its western end to the River Thames and its outline on maps was similar to an old boot – the eastern end of the county from Reading to Windsor occupies, as it were, the arch of the foot and the toe-cap, though the county is now split into several administrative areas based on the large towns of Reading, Bracknell, Maidenhead and Slough.

East Berkshire is far less rural than its western counterpart but in between the main towns and along the southern section of the Thames Valley there is good countryside for walking, as delightful as many far less populated parts. Between Reading and Windsor the Thames has carved a long northerly meander past Henley, Cookham and Maidenhead, where the Thames Path gives easy access to sections along its banks. The M4 cuts through the villages and fields to the south, and beyond the conurbations of Wokingham and Bracknell are the green corridor of the Blackwater River and the substantial expanse of Swinley Forest, equally popular now with walkers, horse-riders and mountain-bikers.

The crowning glory of the county, however, is undoubtedly the town of Windsor, with its world-renowned castle and royal parks giving miles of open space to be explored and enjoyed.

East Berkshire

1. **Cookham and Winter Hill** 76
   Take inspiration from Sir Stanley Spencer's heavenly home village

2. **Hurley and Ashley Hill** 78
   Hike up to higher ground before returning along the Thames

3. **Aston and Remenham** 80
   Loop around the Thames Path with fast-moving rowers for company

4. **Waltham St Lawrence** 82
   Enjoy a level bridleway circuit around quiet park and farmland

5. **Swallowfield and Farley Hill** 84
   Follow riverside paths and hedged lanes on this country walk

6. **Frost Folly Country Park loop** 86
   Explore wildlife-rich meadows, hedgerows and scrubland

7. **Blackwater River and Finchampstead Ridges** 88
   Wander through former gravel pits full of butterflies and dragonflies

8. **Swinley Forest** 90
   March along forest tracks and an old Roman road through a heathland

9. **Windsor and Eton rivers loop** 92
   Stroll the riverside and parkland paths between two historic towns

10. **Windsor Great Park and Virginia Water** 94
    Roam freely through the former deer park packed with interesting sights

EAST BERKSHIRE

Cookham and Winter Hill

Distance 6.5km **Time** 1 hour 45
Terrain riverside and marshland paths
with a steep climb up Winter Hill (the
paths alongside the River Thames and
over Cock Marsh and Cookham Moor are
liable to flooding) **Map** OS Explorer 172
Access bus to Cookham from High
Wycombe and Maidenhead

Cookham sits on the banks of the River
Thames with a Saxon church and extensive
water meadows. It has a close association
with Stanley Spencer, one of the greatest
British painters of the 20th century. He
grew up here and regarded it as a 'village in
heaven'. This walk follows the River
Thames before crossing an ancient marsh
and climbing Winter Hill for some long
views over the Thames Valley.

Walk along the High Street to the
junction with Sutton Road by the Stanley
Spencer Gallery, a former Methodist
chapel, and turn left. Just round the bend
fork left along Church Gate and continue
through the churchyard past Holy Trinity
Church to the River Thames. The route
turns left and follows the Thames Path
for the next 2km. You soon pass Bell Rope
Meadow, where a panel explains its
history as a ropewalk, and then Cookham
Reach Sailing Club to reach a gate onto
the wide expanse of Marsh Meadow. The
opposite bank displays a row of riverside
properties, some developed expansively
from original Victorian mansions, others
of ultra-modern design and a number
sporting Riviera-style boathouses. At the
end of the meadow go through a gate,
opposite which the River Wye flows into
the Thames, and continue along the
eastern edge of Cock Marsh between a
ditch and the river. Pass under the
railway bridge and continue along the
path between houses and the river

COOKHAM AND WINTER HILL

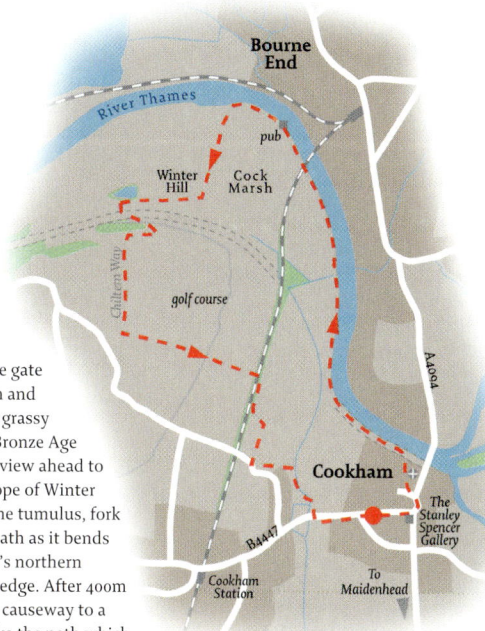

◀ The River Thames near the confluence with the River Wye

where you pass The Bounty pub.

At the end of the houses go through the gate back onto Cock Marsh and bear left along a wide grassy path to a prominent Bronze Age burial mound, with a view ahead to the steep northern slope of Winter Hill. A little beyond the tumulus, fork right and follow the path as it bends right along the marsh's northern boundary fence and hedge. After 400m bear left over a grassy causeway to a footpath junction. Take the path which rises steeply up to the left and gives good views back over the Thames Valley. Near the top of the rise turn sharp right onto a nearly-level path back along the top of the slope. After 150m bear steeply left up to a gate and head along the field edge beyond on the route of the Chiltern Way. At a footpath junction near the end of the field, turn left with the Chiltern Way into Winter Hill Golf Course. The right of way heads downhill, initially beside a fence, and then continues across two fairways, past a works shed and across more fairways to a footbridge over the railway.

On the far side turn right off the Chiltern Way and follow the footpath up the side of this section of the golf course and along a track to a footpath junction just before Terry's Lane. Turn left down the track past Delta House and follow the footpath down the field beyond. Bear right and follow the footpath over the next field beside a stream, Strand Water, to a footbridge into Cookham Moor car park. Cross the B4447 and turn left along the raised causeway back to the High Street in Cookham.

Hurley and Ashley Hill

Distance 8.75km **Time** 2 hours 30
Terrain fields, woods and riverside paths
Map OS Explorer 172 **Access** bus to Hurley from Maidenhead and Henley-on-Thames

The tranquil village of Hurley lies on the banks of the River Thames at an ancient crossing point and ford. There has been a village here since Saxon times and many old buildings survive, strung out along its long High Street. At its northern end you'll find St Mary's Church and the site of a former Benedictine priory. Opposite is Tithecote Manor, a converted tithe barn with a 14th-century dovecote, and Monks' Barn, both originally built for storing the priory's farm produce. This walk takes you to the highest point in East Berkshire before returning along a tranquil stretch of the River Thames.

The walk starts from St Mary's Church, opposite which you'll find the parish council car park. Walk along the High Street through the village to the junction with Henley Road, the A4130. Cross over and take the fenced footpath between fields steeply up Prospect Hill to a path junction by High Wood. Head through the wood back into fields and follow the footpath southwards along a wide grassy strip to reach a track west of Hall Place, which houses Berkshire College of Agriculture. Continue ahead across the field beyond, pass through a wooded dell and follow the edge of the next field to Honey Lane by Lady Place Cottages. The route turns left up the lane past Appletree Cottages and round the right bend. Just before the lane bends back left take the footpath off right on the route of the

Chiltern Way. Follow the waymarks up through the wood, initially along a rough tarmac path and then a track, to the gates to Clifton at the high point of Ashley Hill.

The route bears right here with the Chiltern Way which leads down through the trees, across a bridleway and down to a track. Follow the track down past a cottage and, a little beyond, take the second footpath off left. The Chiltern Way soon bends right down through Channers Plantation to reach a track and footpath junction. You now leave the Chiltern Way, which turns sharp left, and keep ahead down the track. Just beyond, a bridleway joins the track and in another 150m, where the track ends, continue ahead on the undulating bridleway along a grassy, hedged strip to a gate into a nature reserve managed by the Berkshire, Buckinghamshire and Oxfordshire Wildlife Trust. The bridleway heads down through the wooded reserve to a bridleway junction, where a right fork takes you out of the trees and down to Henley Road again.

Cross over and dogleg briefly right along the pavement and then left onto an enclosed footpath which takes you between fields towards the houses at Frogmill. At the end of the fields dogleg to the left down a passageway to reach the River Thames. The final section of the walk turns right and follows the waymarked Thames Path for a little over 1.5km, initially along a track past houses and then over riverside meadows past Hurley Weir to Hurley Lock. To visit the lock, you can cross the footbridge over the river channel. To return directly to the start, turn right at the bridge and head along the passageway between houses to the northern end of Hurley.

◀ On Prospect Hill looking back over the Thames Valley

Aston and Remenham

Distance 5km **Time** 1 hour 15
Terrain riverside path, lanes and fields
(the Thames Path between Aston and
Remenham, as well as Ferry Lane car park
itself, is liable to flooding)
Map OS Explorer 171 **Access** no public
transport to the start

**The secluded village of Aston lies
northeast of Henley surrounded by fields
under the lee of Remenham Hill where
there was an ancient ferry across the river.
The walk, in a loop of the River Thames,
passes by Hambleden Lock and along the
upper part of the rowing course of Henley
Royal Regatta to the village of Remenham.**

The walk starts from the bottom of Ferry Lane, where there is a small but popular public parking area by the River Thames. It would also be possible to start the walk along the route at Remenham, where parking is possible by the church, or at the Flowerpot Hotel in Aston if the intention is to visit. The first part of the walk follows the Thames Path left out of the Ferry Lane parking area and heads over the riverside meadow. At the far end go through a gate onto a tarmac track and follow it to Hambleden Weir and Lock. On the opposite bank is Hambleden Mill, an historic watermill built for grinding flour and now converted into flats. The lock was also the location for the start of the original Oxford and Cambridge Boat Race in 1829 before the course was transferred to London.

Continue past the lock over the meadow beyond and follow the Thames Path around the sweeping left bend, where you

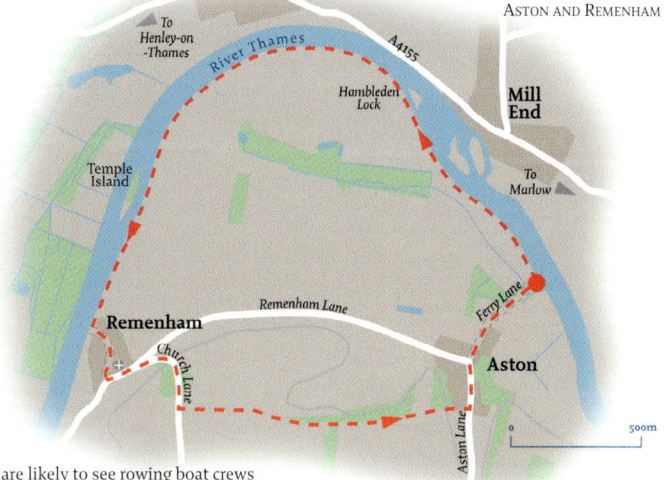

are likely to see rowing boat crews ploughing up and down. The white mansion on the opposite bank is called Greenlands and was built for the bookseller and newsagent WH Smith in 1853. Round the bend you pass Temple Island, which gets its name from the neoclassical rotunda temple at its southern end. This was designed by James Wyatt in 1771 as a folly for Fawley Court on the Henley side of the river and also serves as a well-known landmark at the start of the course for Henley Royal Regatta, held here each year in July since 1839.

Continue along the towpath past Temple Island Meadows and after another 400m, just beyond the rear entrance to Remenham Manor, leave the Thames Path and take the footpath off left. Go along the walled permissive path which passes through Remenham Farm up to St Nicholas' Church in Remenham. In pre-Christian times the area was associated with the Saxon god Woden, whose symbol was the raven, and the village's unusual name is thought to mean 'home of the ravens'. Inside the church on the north wall is a commemorative plaque to John, Lord Hunt, leader of the first ascent of Mount Everest in 1953, who lived in the parish for many years.

At the junction with Remenham Lane dogleg left along it for just under 100m and then fork right steeply up Remenham Church Lane. After the gradient eases look out for a footpath off left which carries the Chiltern Way. This waymarked path takes you along an undulating track between fields and then a path along the top of a wooded bank. You then head downhill between a house and an orchard to reach Aston Lane. Turn left down the lane to the centre of Aston and at the Flowerpot Hotel bear right down Ferry Lane to the river and the car park.

◀ The rotunda on Temple Island

Waltham St Lawrence

Distance 7km **Time** 1 hour 45
Terrain waymarked byways, lanes and fields **Map** OS Explorer 159 or 160
Access bus to Waltham St Lawrence from Maidenhead

The village of Waltham St Lawrence has undergone considerable expansion in recent times, but despite this the heart of this attractive village is still centred around its small green. On one side is the 12th-century St Lawrence Church and on the other is a 15th-century pub, The Bell. This is a more or less level walk and for much of the way follows the waymarked Knowl Hill Bridleway Circuit along old byways and quiet lanes in the heart of East Berkshire.

From the green, walk along Milley Road past the 16th-century Neville Hall towards the western edge of the village. After just under 500m, opposite The Dene, fork left with Knowl Hill Bridleway Circuit and follow the restricted byway of Nut Lane between fields to Twyford Road. The Bridleway Circuit crosses the road, heads left along the grass verge to the bend and then bears right along a restricted byway past houses. Initially a track and then a tree-lined path, the byway winds its way between fields to emerge into Mire Lane. Continue ahead along the lane past West End Farm to the junction with Plough Lane. Turn left along Plough Lane and, after 150m, bear right along Bailey's Lane, where you pass brick-timbered Bailey's Cottage. Continue ahead, go round the left bend and then turn right along Brook Lane. After 100m, at the bend, the Bridleway Circuit forks left along another restricted byway called Uncle's Lane. This passes between fields and after 700m reaches the road at Shurlock Row.

Turn left along the road for 100m over a stream to the junction beyond. The Bridleway Circuit briefly doglegs sharply

◀ The lake in Shottesbrooke Park

right and then left along another pleasant byway. After just over 1km, where the byway bends left, the route temporarily leaves the Bridleway Circuit and continues in the same direction onto a footpath. This takes you across the field ahead, through a spinney and down a track to Broadmoor Road. Cross over the road and rejoin the Bridleway Circuit, which now enters the parkland of Shottesbrooke Park. Head past the lake and the house to the church. The house, a private residence, in part dates from Tudor times and the neighbouring church's octagonal spire is modelled on that of Salisbury Cathedral.

At this point you leave the Bridleway Circuit and turn left onto a footpath which leads between the church and the house. Continue ahead through a brick archway and along a walled section shaded by yew trees to a gate into fields. Follow the footpath along the edges of two parkland fields to Halls Lane.

The final part of the route turns right along the lane and after 300m, by Halls Farm House, forks left along a footpath. Go past the burial ground and pass between houses and gardens to rejoin Halls Lane, where a left turn takes you back to the village centre and the start.

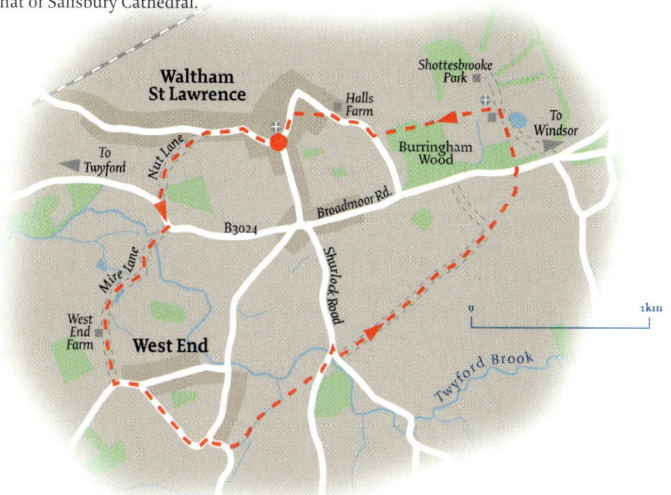

Swallowfield and Farley Hill

Distance 10.5km **Time** 2 hours 45
Terrain riverside and field paths, lanes and byways **Map** OS Explorer 159
Access bus to Swallowfield from Reading

This is a varied country walk through the parkland and farmland of the Farley Estate in the Blackwater Valley with a return over the higher ground on which the spread-out village of Farley Hill stands. The walk starts from the village of Swallowfield which lies a few miles south of Reading not far from the border with Hampshire.

From the roundabout by the war memorial and the village hall, walk along Church Road and turn left through the pedestrian gate by the cattle grid onto a permissive path into Swallowfield Park. The park and house have been in existence since the mid-1500s and are today the site for the Swallowfield Show, held here in August each year. Head over the field and bend right to the bridge over the Blackwater River. Cross the bridge and turn right along the permissive path beside the river to All Saints Church. Bear left up through the churchyard past the east end of the church and turn right along the permissive path over Swallowfield Park's driveway to a gate onto the public footpath.

Turn left and follow the fenced footpath to a path junction at the end of the field and turn right to reach Church Road. The route doglegs right down the road and then left just before the bend, along

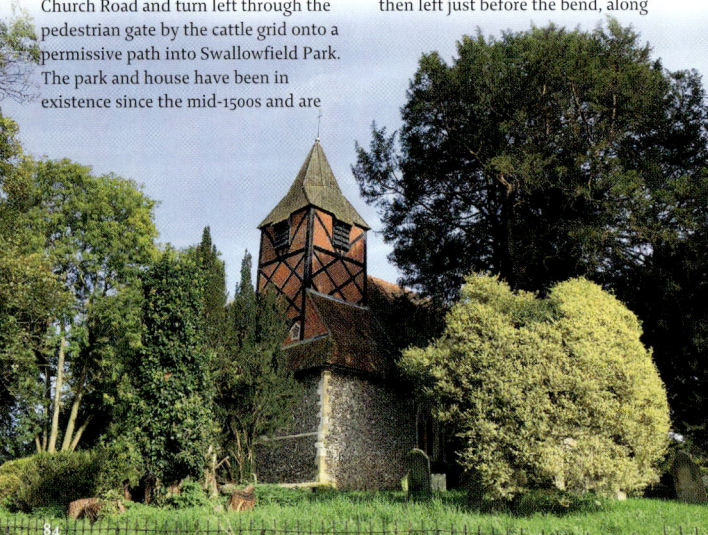

Swallowfield and Farley Hill

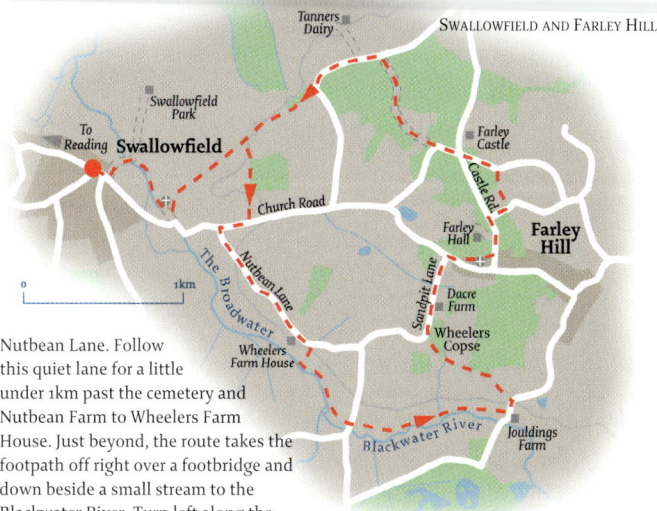

Nutbean Lane. Follow this quiet lane for a little under 1km past the cemetery and Nutbean Farm to Wheelers Farm House. Just beyond, the route takes the footpath off right over a footbridge and down beside a small stream to the Blackwater River. Turn left along the riverside path to Ford Lane, across which the footpath continues along the edge of four fields, at times near the river, to the lane by Jouldings Farm.

Turn left up the lane and, at the bend, bear left onto a byway which winds its way up to Sandpit Lane. Turn right along this undulating lane past Dacre Farm and up to the junction at Bungler's Hill. The route bears right across the road past the southern entrance to Farley Hall and along a byway behind Farley Hill's church, now a private house. At the road turn left, go round the left bend and turn right along Church Lane. Just past the cricket club take the footpath off left, at first beside the cricket ground and then some woodland. Turn left along the next lane past a watertower to the crossroads at Castle Hill just up from the entrance to Farley Castle, a country house dating from the early 1800s and built in Gothic style with battlements and turrets.

Cross over, walk along the Swallowfield road to the bend and take the byway ahead along a track. At the fork by Kiln House keep left to continue along the byway, which soon heads downhill through trees to reach Swallowfield Road. Turn left along the road to the sweeping left bend, where a little care is needed to watch out for any oncoming traffic. Once round the bend take the footpath off right which leads between the fields of Swallowfield Park. After just over 500m you arrive back at the path junction reached on the outward route at the end of the field near All Saints Church.

From here, retrace your steps past the church and onto the permissive path along the Blackwater River to bring you back to Swallowfield.

◀ All Saints Church, Swallowfield

Frost Folly Country Park loop

Distance 7.5km **Time** 2 hours
Terrain fields, lanes and byways
Map OS Explorer 160 **Access** bus from Bracknell to Moss End stops on Maidenhead Road, the A3095, at the junction with the western end of Bowyer's Lane, 500m from the start

This walk sets out from the delightful Frost Folly Country Park which lies between the villages of Moss End and Warfield in the countryside to the north of Bracknell. This small park contains a variety of habitats, including wildlife meadows, hedgerow, scrubland and several small ponds. It's also a good place to spot farmland birds, such as skylarks, goldfinches, swallows and red kites. Many of the pathways here are created naturally by cutting the wildflower meadows in summer for hay.

The walk starts from Frost Folly Country Park's car park located 500m east of Moss End along Bowyer's Lane. Head out the back of the car park and follow the surfaced trail which passes along the left edge of the park and then winds its way to the right down to a pond. Turn left past the pond, climb gently uphill along the track beyond and turn right through a gate to reach Church Lane in Warfield opposite the church.

Turn left along the lane and in just under 100m take the footpath off right down three fields. Cross a footbridge over The Cut stream and bear left through some poplar woodland beside the stream to the road at Wane Bridge. The route doglegs left up the road for just over 100m and right into the parking area for Windmill Meadows. Pass along the left edge of the first meadow to a gate onto

Frost Folly Country Park loop

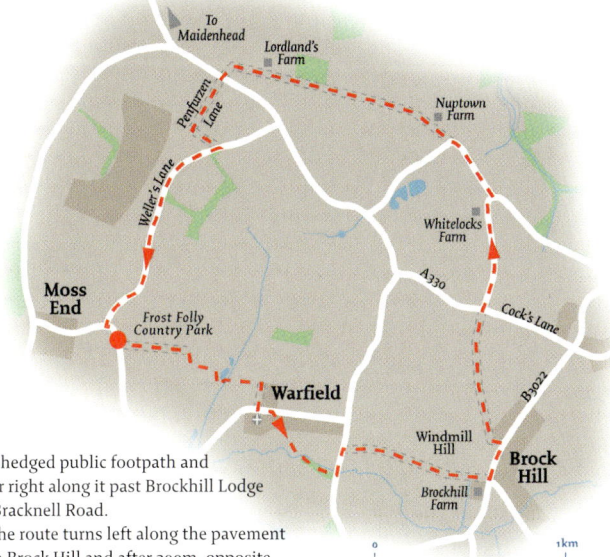

the hedged public footpath and bear right along it past Brockhill Lodge to Bracknell Road.

The route turns left along the pavement into Brock Hill and after 200m, opposite Planners Farm, turns left onto a footpath. Follow the footpath beside a fence and then bear right with it through a gate into fields. You now follow the footpath along a wide grassy strip with fields on the left and pass through two more gates to reach the A330. Cross over and follow narrow Garsons Lane past houses to the junction on the bend by Whitelocks Farm. Turn left along Hawthorn Lane, another pleasant country lane, and after 300m at the bend into Nuptown Lane keep ahead along Hawthorn Lane. This old lane soon becomes a byway track and heads uphill past Nuptown Farm. Follow the track, lined by some sturdy oak trees, over the slight rise. Keep on past two byways off left and further on pass the entrances to Lordland's Farm and Fernygrove Farm to reach the A330 again.

Cross over and follow Penfurzen Lane byway ahead, which after 300m bends left to reach Weller's Lane. The final part of the walk turns right here and follows the lane round the bend, where it soon narrows and winds its way for just under 1km past Weller's Wood and between fields back to the entrance to Frost Folly Country Park.

◂ Autumn meadows in Frost Folly Country Park

Blackwater River and Finchampstead Ridges

Distance 5.5km **Time** 1 hour 30
Terrain riverside, woodland and lakeside paths with one moderate climb
Map OS Explorer 159 or 160
Access no public transport to the start

This short but varied walk starts from Horseshoe Lake and takes you beside the Blackwater River and Moor Green Lakes Nature Reserve. The lakes here are former gravel pits and are now home to a range of wildlife, including wildfowl and wading birds. The surrounding meadows are rich with flowers in summer, attracting butterflies and dragonflies, and you may see the flash of a kingfisher along the Blackwater River. The second half of the route provides a contrast and takes you up over the higher ground of Finchampstead Ridges, a common of ancient heath and woodland.

The walk starts from Bracknell Forest Council's Horseshoe Lake car park off Mill Lane near Sandhurst. Head out the rear of the car park and bear left through trees for 150m along the Blackwater Valley Path to a path junction in front of the Blackwater River. The route turns right here with the Blackwater Valley Path which winds its way alongside the river, with Horseshoe Lake off to the right through the trees. After 600m bend left, past the permissive path off right along the western end of Horseshoe Lake, and continue beside the river, with Moor Green Lakes Nature Reserve on the right. In 1km pass a footbridge and keep ahead for another 100m to a path junction. Leave the Blackwater Valley Path here and turn right along the footpath past Colebrook Lakes and through a parking area to Lower Sandhurst Road.

◀ Looking across to Bird Island on Horseshoe Lake

The route now turns right along the road past houses and mansions. In 400m, at Moor Green House, take the restricted bridleway off left to climb up past The Old Thatch into woodland. The byway climbs steadily into Finchampstead Ridges, descends across a small dip just past the last house and then rises more steeply to a path junction at a high point.

Turn right off the byway and follow the footpath alongside paling through the mixed woodland to its far edge. Bend right with the footpath down out of the wood and continue between fields along the northern edge of Beech Hill, which is crowned with a covering of trees. Continue to follow the path down the hill's eastern side, now with woodland on the left. The path then bends left down into the trees of Coalpit Copse and heads up to Ambarrow Lane.

Turn left along the lane and after 100m, just before the bend, turn right through a gate onto a footpath into fields, signed for Horseshoe Lake. Descend the right-hand edges of three fields beside a small stream to reach Lower Sandhurst Road again. Cross over and follow the path ahead along the eastern edge of Horseshoe Lake past Bird Island, whose shape gives the lake its name, and the activity centre to the council car park at the start.

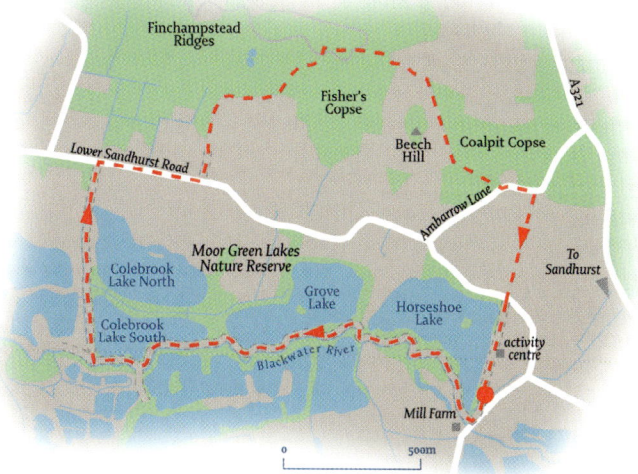

Swinley Forest

Distance 6km (incl short detour)
Time 1 hour 30 **Terrain** forest tracks and paths **Map** OS Explorer 160
Access no public transport to the start

Swinley Forest is an extensive area of heathland and woodland hills to the south of Bracknell. This walk heads for the oldest area of the forest where it passes along a short stretch of The Devil's Highway, a former Roman road from London to Silchester. Nearby you'll find 'Caesar's Camp' which, despite the name, is a large Iron Age fort. Its earthworks have been dated to more than 600 years before Julius Caesar invaded Britain and the fort's inhabitants are most likely to have been the Atrebates tribe, whose capital was at Silchester.

The walk starts from The Look Out Discovery Centre, located off Nine Mile Road, the B3430, on the southern edge of Bracknell. There is a large car park, picnic and play area, and a café with outdoor seating. In recent years Swinley Forest has become a popular location for mountain bikers as well as walkers, and can get very busy at weekends. However, once you venture a little away from the start, the crowds thin out, though it's worth keeping an eye and ear out for mountain bikers, whose graded trails cross some of the main forest tracks and paths.

From the car park and picnic area follow signs for the Ramblers Route along the left side of the building housing the Discovery Centre and Woodlarks Café to a gate onto a track. Cross the track and bear half-right along a path to the next junction. Turn left with the Ramblers Route and climb the wide track up the north side of Gravel Hill. At the top continue ahead past the triangulation pillar and keep on along the track which winds its way through the pine

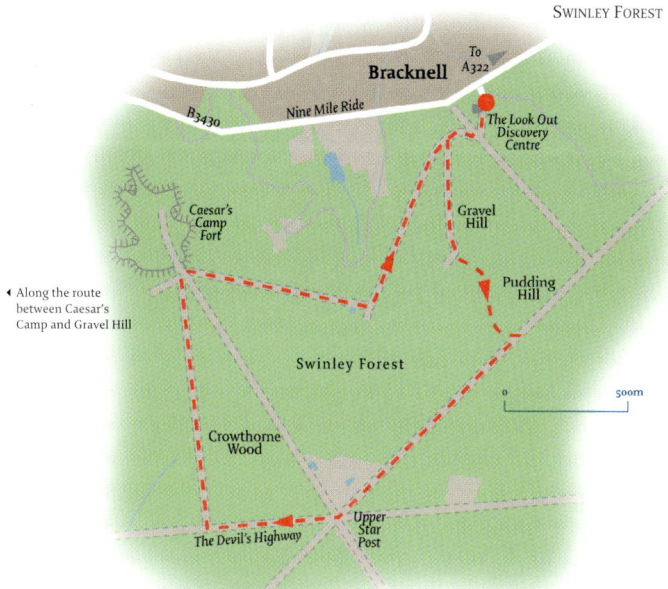

◄ Along the route between Caesar's Camp and Gravel Hill

plantation to a crosspaths just out of the trees at Pudding Hill. Keep ahead for 75m to the next junction and turn right, signed for the Ramblers Route. The walk heads along the wide straight ride between an old plantation on the left and a younger one on the right. After 1km, just past some covered reservoirs, you reach Upper Star Post, a junction of six tracks. Keep ahead half-right with the Ramblers Route along the track called The Devil's Highway.

After 500m, at the next crosspaths, you leave the Ramblers Route and turn right along a narrower path. This takes you northwards for 1km between denser plantations, past Wickham Bushes, a nature conservation area, and through Crowthorne Wood to the junction in front of Caesar's Camp. You can venture into the middle of the Iron Age fort by going through the gate and following the path northwards for about 300m.

The onward route turns right along the track signed for The Look Out through trees, over a cross-track and then along an undulating section between older and younger plantations. At the next junction, just past the small Forest Pond, turn left onto a wide track along the western side of Gravel Hill, past The Summit mountain bike area and over the rise beyond. Continue down to the next cross-track, beyond which lies the path back to The Look Out Discovery Centre.

EAST BERKSHIRE

Windsor and Eton rivers loop

Distance 8.25km **Time** 2 hours
Terrain town streets, surfaced tracks and riverside path **Map** OS Explorer 160
Access bus to Windsor from Maidenhead, Slough and Reading; train to Windsor from London, Reading and Slough

Windsor is often first on many a tourist's list of places to visit outside of London, whether to see its famous castle, take a boat cruise on the River Thames, glimpse royal residents or the tailcoated pupils of Eton College, or spend the day at nearby Legoland. The Royal Borough of Windsor also contains some beautiful countryside, much of it managed by the National Trust and the Crown Estate.

This walk, a blend of town and country, crosses the River Thames and heads along Eton's High Street before looping round alongside the Jubilee River and returning through The Home Park along the Thames Path.

From the centre of Windsor, walk down the High Street into Thames Street and alongside the wall of Windsor Castle. Bend right past the theatre and then left over Datchet Road to Windsor Bridge. Cross this pedestrianised bridge over the River Thames and continue along Eton High Street. Keep ahead into Slough Road past Eton College Chapel and fork left along Common Lane. At the end of the buildings continue along the lane, which carries a footpath, over the Colenorton Brook and, at the bend, fork left to the railway line. The route passes under the railway and turns right beside its embankment. Pass under the A332 and turn right back under the railway and alongside the Jubilee River, past a weir and footbridge, to Slough Road. Cross over at the pelican crossing and

The River Thames at Windsor Bridge

continue along a wooded path beside the Jubilee River to the next footbridge.

The route turns right onto a footpath along an avenue of lime trees between playing fields of Eton College to Pococks Lane. Cross over and turn left along the pavement to the bend. Fork right onto the footpath which passes between some boathouses and the River Thames, over scrubby ground and across a footbridge over the Jubilee River.

On the far side turn right alongside the river and under the railway into Datchet Golf Course. Head along the side of the fairway and then a tree-lined track to a green on the right. Just past the green turn right across a ditch up steps to Windsor Road and then right along the pavement over the Victoria Bridge. Continue to the end of the railings and turn right into The Home Park. This park was originally an extensive garden between Windsor Castle and the River Thames, but in 1851 Queen Victoria decreed that it should be given over to the public as a place of recreation.

The route now follows the Thames Path back to Windsor. Head across the field to the river and turn left along the tree-fringed riverside path to the railway. Pass under the railway bridge and continue round the river bend past the northern end of Romney Island to reach the boatyard at Romney Lock. Follow the waymarks through the boatyard and continue along its entrance road beside the railway. Before Riverside Station's car park fork right onto the riverside path between railings. This path takes you past Riverside Station and along Thames Side to Windsor Bridge, where a left turn will bring you back up into Windsor.

Windsor Great Park and Virginia Water

Distance 8.5km **Time** 2 hour 15
Terrain surfaced parkland paths
Map OS Explorer 160 **Access** no public transport to the start

Windsor Great Park is one of the oldest royal parks in the country and dates back to Saxon times. This walk starts from The Savill Garden in the southern part of the park and completes a circuit of Virginia Water. It passes many well-known features such as the Cascade, the Cumberland Obelisk, the Totem Pole, the Ruins of Leptis Magna, the Five Arch Bridge and The Valley Gardens. Along the route are plenty of panels which help explain the park's history.

From the time of the Normans the area was enclosed as a deer park, or forest, for hunting. Many of the most iconic parts of the park were created from the time of the Restoration, including The Long Walk, the famous 4km-long tree-lined avenue to Windsor Castle. This walk passes alongside Virginia Water which was created by William Augustus, Duke of Cumberland and youngest son of George II, and at the time was the largest man-made lake in England. In 1752 the Duke embarked on transforming this part of the park into a royal pleasure ground and his work was continued by George IV and Queen Victoria. In 1932 George V commissioned the creation of the park's first garden. George VI later renamed this The Savill Garden in honour of its creator, Eric Savill.

The walk starts from the car park at The Savill Garden. In front of the visitor centre turn left and follow Rhododendron Ride, signed for Virginia Water, to the Cumberland Obelisk. Continue down the surfaced ride past Obelisk Lawn and bend right along the causeway past the eastern

Windsor Great Park and Virginia Water

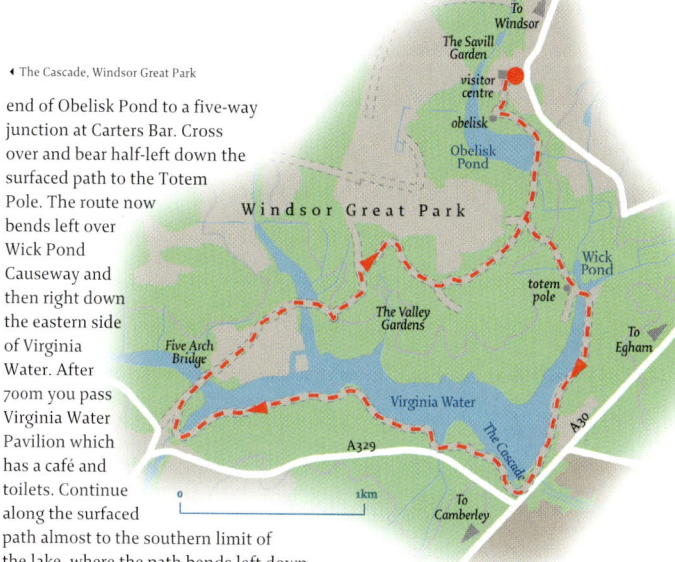

◀ The Cascade, Windsor Great Park

end of Obelisk Pond to a five-way junction at Carters Bar. Cross over and bear half-left down the surfaced path to the Totem Pole. The route now bends left over Wick Pond Causeway and then right down the eastern side of Virginia Water. After 700m you pass Virginia Water Pavilion which has a café and toilets. Continue along the surfaced path almost to the southern limit of the lake, where the path bends left down into a dip by The Cascade.

Walk uphill above the Cascade to the Leptis Magna ruins, a classical folly built from materials taken from the ancient Roman city in present-day Libya. The route now heads along the southern edge of the lake for 1.5km, past a viewpoint across the lake to The Fishing Temple, and bends right over its southwestern arm to reach the drive over Five Arch Bridge. Cross the bridge, continue up the pedestrian path beside the drive and cross the bridge over the western arm of the lake. At the junction beyond bear right uphill into The Valley Gardens.

At the first junction fork left uphill to the top of the rise and continue ahead on the surfaced path which winds its way above Pinetum Valley to a gate on the right into the Heather Garden. Follow the path through the garden to a gate at its far end onto a five-way path junction. Take the surfaced path ahead, signed for The Savill Garden, past public toilets over to the left, and go down the slope past Money Hill out of The Valley Gardens. The route now follows the undulating path above Darkhole, down on the right, to reach the five-way junction at Carters Bar. From here, cross over and retrace your steps past Obelisk Pond and back up to The Savill Garden.

Index

Adstock	18
Ashley Hill	78
Aston	80
Aston Abbotts	48
Biddlesden	10
Bledlow	40
Black Park Country Park	72
Blackwater River	88
Boarstall	32
Botley	58
Bracknell	90
Bradenham	66
Brill	32
Buckland Common	54
Burnham Beeches	70
Chackmore	12
Chalfont St Giles	62
Chenies	60
Chesham	58
Cholesbury	54
Cookham	76
Coombe Hill	46
Cublington	48
Cuddington	38
Dunsmore	46
Egypt Woods	70
Eton	92
Farley Hill	84
Finchampstead Ridges	88
Fingest	68
Frost Folly Country Park	86
Great Brickhill	28
Great Hampden	56
Great Horwood	18
Hambleden Valley	68
Hillesden	16
Hurley	78
Ivinghoe Beacon	50
Lodge Hill	40
Milton Keynes	26
Moss End	86
Nether Winchendon	38
Penn Wood	64
Princes Risborough	42
Quainton Hill	34
Ravenstone	22
Remenham	80
Sherington	24
Slough	72, 92
Steeple Claydon	16
Stoke Hammond	28
Stowe Gardens	12
Swallowfield	84
Swinley Forest	90
Thornborough	20
Tingewick	14
Tyler's Hill	58
Tyringham	24
Virginia Water	94
Waddesdon	36
Waltham St Lawrence	82
Warfield	86
Water Stratford	14
Wendover Woods	44
Westcott	36
Weston Underwood	22
West Wycombe	66
Whiteleaf Hill	42
Willen Lake	26
Winchmore Hill	64
Windsor	92
Windsor Great Park	94
Wing	48
Winter Hill	76